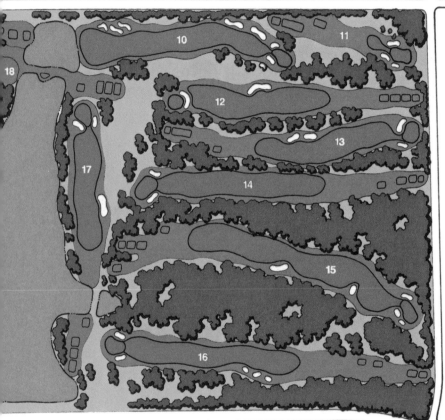

WHERE BOBBY LEARNED TO PLAY

WHERE BOBBY LEARNED TO PLAY

— East Lake Golf Club in Atlanta —

The Home Course of
Bobby Jones is Full of Memories

LINTON C. HOPKINS

McGuire Publishing Company, Inc.
Atlanta, Georgia

PERMISSIONS

The author and publisher wish to express their thanks to the following for the use of copyrighted material. To Doubleday-Dell Publishers for material from *Bobby Jones on Golf, Golf is My Game,* and *The Basic Golf Swing*; to Martin Elgison, Alston and Bird, and the family of Bobby Jones for portions of *Down the Fairway* and for photographs of Bobby Jones; to Charlie Elliott and Cherokee Publishers for quotations from *The East Lake Country Club History*; to Simon and Schuster for part of one story from *Harvey Penick's Little Red Book*; to the *Atlanta Journal and Constitution* for use of the 1922 article on the 63 by Bobby Jones, by O.B. Keeler, and for the excerpt from the article on the 1963 Ryder Cup by Ed Miles; to the memory of O.B. Keeler and W. Foulsham & Co., New York for material from *The Bobby Jones Story* and excerpts from *The Greatest*; to William Morrow & Co. for *The Legend of Bagger Vance*; to Fred Russell and A.S. Barnes & Co. for *Bury Me In An Old Press Box*; to *Golf Journal* and the United States Golf Association for photographs of Jim Barnes, Joyce Wethered, Tom Cousins, and Charlie Yates; to *Georgia Trend* for a photograph of Robert Woodruff and Bobby Jones; to Rees Jones for the use of the schematic plan of his redesign of the holes at East Lake; to *Golf Magazine*; to Ailsa Publications and the memory of Bernard Darwin for *Golf Between Two Wars*; to Herbert Warren Wind for an excerpt from one of his wonderful pieces on Jones (reprinted by permission, © 1976 Herbert Warren Wind, originally in *The New Yorker*, all rights reserved); to *The New York Times* for the obituary of Bobby Jones, Dec. 19, 1971; and to the Associated Press, for excerpts from *The New York Times*, Dec. 19, 1971.

Published by
McGuire Publishing Company, Inc.
540 High Point Lane
Atlanta, Georgia 30342

Second edition, First printing (1998)

Printed in the United States of America

ISBN 0-9628381-1-X

Cover and text design by Tonya Beach.
Book development by Bookmark, Atlanta, Georgia.

TO THE READER

*I*t seems necessary to explain my use of *Bobby* instead of *Bob* throughout this book. Usually, those who don't know someone named *Robert* call him Bob, avoiding the more informal Bobby for fear of seeming too familiar. We assume that his family and friends use Bobby, and we don't wish to intrude. However, for Robert Tyre Jones, Jr., as you will learn, *Little Bob* or Bob was intimate; Bobby was only used by his public.

Bernard Darwin, the greatest golf writer of Jones' day, called him "The Immortal Bobby." Herbert Warren Wind, the greatest writer on golf in the modern era, knew him first from a distance and used Bobby, but when he became a friend he always spoke of Bob. All of the books about him, including his own, used the name known by the world, not the one used by his family and circle of friends.

Today, when someone calls him Bob you can assume that the person speaking was a friend, since he preferred that term be used by those who were close to him. But for the rest of us who never knew him, and in Britain, and wherever golf is played, he will always be what the people of Scotland named him when they first took him into their hearts in the 1920's. . . . "our Bobby."

The Author

CONTENTS

INTRODUCTION

*I*n the late twentieth century, Bobby Jones belongs to history. To the younger generation of golfers he seems almost as distant as the gutta-percha ball. Everyone knows that he was a great golfer and began the Masters tournament, but it is rare to meet an active golfer who is able to recount even the skeleton of his career.

The printed record shows a lot more. All of the victories are well documented, and *Down the Fairway*, *The Bobby Jones Story, Golf is My Game*, and *Bobby Jones on Golf* are on the shelves of everyone who has tried to look below the surface and understand who he was.

But the literature is incomplete in two respects. The first concerns the ground which he called "my golf course," the eighteen holes at East Lake. This 180 acres is the piece of earth known more intimately by him than any other. Looking at it another way, these few holes, and the older course underneath, which lived from 1908 to 1913, hold more information on him than any other place. Except for two men named Tom Morris and the Old Course at St. Andrews, there is no stronger bond between a legendary golfer and one golf course.

Something about a golf course holds onto history as well as an old house or farm. Tennis courts and many modern baseball parks are standardized and featureless. If you've played on one, you've played them all. But every golf course is unique. Old courses are completely different from one another, even if the setting is similar. No one who has played the Old Course at St. Andrews and Prestwick, Troon, and Muirfield ever mentions how similar they are, except to call them "links land." The same is true of the older American courses. Every tee, trap, and green knows things that have happened nowhere else; and since each place is unique, special events are easy to remember.

For Bobby Jones, that *house* and *farm* are at East Lake. This is why it seems important to make the effort to find out where everything was when he was there, and learn exactly where he worked his magic.

Secondly, when his life is studied, the importance of his family and friends rises to the top. But no attempt has been made to interview the members of his family in the preparation of this book. Details from the family of a great man belong to them, and any stories they tell to someone outside the family must, in some way, intrude upon their privacy. Most of us are reluctant to talk too much about members of our immediate family. We want to cherish our memories and keep them to ourselves; they underscore our relationship and give us private pleasure. If someone else has them, they own a piece of us, which is always slightly uncomfortable. If a family member decides one day that the time is right to record what they know, the world will have a treat, but the time and method should be their decision.

In contrast, friends touched by greatness seem to feel an obligation to instruct the rest of us. Friends worry that their little pieces of immortality will be lost, and they want to make sure that their stories survive, and that we get them right.

These are the purposes of this volume. First, we wish to present the golf course at East Lake as the place that Bobby knew best. Equally important is to collect and record the memories of his friends — to set down in one place everything that's come out so far.

I

A Round At East Lake
With Bobby Jones
and His Father and Friends

$\mathcal{T}$o most golfers, the word *Georgia* means the television images of Augusta National, home of the Masters. To most Georgians, golf means one or more of the hundreds of private and public courses that seem to be springing up in the mountains, Piedmont, and coastal regions of the largest state east of the Mississippi. But to those who play at East Lake, golf means the gently rolling ground where Bobby Jones played all of his active life. This is the course that Donald Ross created in 1913, when the man with "poetry in his swing" was a boy of eleven.

The first golf course at East Lake, also the first eighteen-hole course in Atlanta, was designed by Tom Bendelow between 1906 and 1908. That original course occupied the young Jones until age eleven, when in 1913, Donald Ross completely reworked the layout into the basic design of today. Before 1963, the Ross course was altered for the Ryder Cup by George Cobb. Most of the holes were lengthened, many bunkers were added, and all the greens were rebuilt and changed from Bermuda to bent grass. Finally, in 1994, Tom Cousins and Rees Jones worked their magic; the course was modernized, brought up to tip-top shape, and returned to the feel of Donald Ross, with all new greens, fairways, and bunkers. The changes add interest — those who know the details enjoy pointing all of them out.

As a boy and young man, Bobby also played in Atlanta at Brookhaven, the course of the Capital City Club, at Ansley Golf Club, and Druid Hills Golf Club. When he escaped to the cool North Carolina mountains he played at Highlands Country Club. After his retirement in 1930, he became associated with other golf courses. He was the founder of the Augusta National Golf Club and designed its wonderful course with Dr. Alister MacKenzie in 1931 and 1932. Also, he founded Peachtree Golf Club in 1948 and built its course with Robert Trent Jones. In addition, his name will always be closely associated with the courses that saw his great victories. St. Andrews, Hoylake, Interlachen, and Merion were the sites of the Grand Slam in 1930, and there are many, many more, throughout America and Great Britain.

However, no golf course can claim the soul of

Bobby Jones to the same extent as East Lake. It saw the start of his golfing life at age five and his last round at forty-six. In between, he walked the course with his father and friends during his childhood, his competitive career, and for sixteen years after he retired. For forty-one years, East Lake was the course he played more than any other. He was world famous for twenty-five of those years and could have played anywhere, but day after day he came back home to East Lake to be with his father and friends.

All who have studied the life of Bobby Jones know of his devotion to his friends and golfing companions and many of his quotes attest to this quality. When he accepted the honor of Freedom of the City of St. Andrews in 1958, the only American since Benjamin Franklin to be so honored, he gave a short speech. In *Golf is My Game*, a chapter called "St. Andrews — A Short Love Story" includes the following words on friendship.

Then it occurred to me to speak of my interpretation of the words 'friend' and 'friendship,' which are among the most important in our language, and yet are so often loosely used. Friends are a man's priceless treasures, and a life rich in friendship is full indeed. When I say, with due regard for the meaning of the word, that I am your friend, I have pledged to you the ultimate in loyalty and devotion. In some respects friendship may even transcend love, for in true friendship there is no place for jealousy. When, without more, I say that you are my friends it is possible that I may be imposing upon you a greater burden than you are willing to assume. But when you have made me aware on many occasions that you have a kindly feeling toward me, and when you have honored me by every means at your command, and when I call you friend, I am at once affirming my high regard and affection for you and declaring my complete faith in you and trust in the sincerity of your expressions. And so, my fellow citizens of St. Andrews, it is with this appreciation of the full sense of the word that I salute you as my friends.

Today the stories of several of his friends are able to connect us to him and to his golf course. Watts Gunn was co-finalist with Bobby at the 1925 U.S. Amateur and a former Georgia Amateur and NCAA champion.[1] Charlie Yates is a longtime member of the Atlanta Athletic Club, Peachtree Golf Club, and the Augusta National Golf Club, and has been one of the hosts at the Masters for many years. He is the 1938 British Amateur champion and grew up at East Lake in a house just off the fourth tee. East Lake is the only course in history which has produced two British Amateur champions, Bobby Jones in 1930

---

[1] Watts Gunn died at age eighty-nine on November 5, 1994.

and Charlie Yates in 1938.

Just before the final, on May 27, 1938, Charlie was handed a telegram:

"To Charlie Yates at Troon. East Lake, Atlanta, America. Pulling hard partner. Come through. — Bob Jones."

Charlie Elliott is the retired sportsman and author who was Bobby's longtime golfing friend and favorite hunting and fishing companion. Dr. Cyrus Strickler was a retired Atlanta internist who played many friendly rounds with Bobby. Richard Courts was an Atlanta business leader who knew Bobby and his father for many years.[2] Mariana Goldsmith Eager is a former East Lake swimming champion who moved out to East Lake from town every summer between 1910 and 1922.

In 1993, at age seventy-seven, Tommy Barnes, the youngest of Bobby's golfing friends, was the only one who still played every day at East Lake. Remarkably, Tommy is also the owner of the lowest round ever shot at East Lake. In 1989, at age seventy-three, Tommy shot a 62 and holds the course record on the Ryder Cup course (1963-1994). Bobby shot a 63 at age twenty in 1922, which is the course record on the Donald Ross course (1914-1960). These two rounds in the low 60's, at ages twenty and seventy-three, mean

---

2 Richard W. Courts died on December 31, 1992 at age ninety-six.
Dr. Cyrus W. Strickler, Jr. died at age ninety-one on May 28, 1998.

that East Lake may be the site of the two best rounds in golfing history at the extremes of ages.

During the thirties and forties, his friends at East Lake saw a lot of Bobby Jones. Tommy recalls: "Bob played out here every day he was in town, usually with his father. They were real close." On August 18, 1948, Tommy played with Bobby at East Lake in his last round of golf: "We played the back nine first that day and Bob played well up to the next to last hole. Then he hooked his drive on number eight into the woods and sort of shuffled off the tee. He went into the hospital for tests the next day. He never played again."[3]

Although Bobby played many rounds at East Lake every year from 1908 through 1948, only one remains intact in sufficient detail to connect him to the golfer of today. The lowest round of his career, the course record nine under par 63, was written up in *The Atlanta Journal* by O.B. Keeler on September 17, 1922, the day after it occurred. Because of this newspaper article, it's possible to play today with the details in mind and imagine that Bobby is there. The length of your drive and the choice on your approach can be compared to what he did. This experience can be enjoyed best at East Lake.

Before beginning to play, we should pause and think about the golf holes he helped design. In the same way that his films and books are his visual and verbal legacy, the thirty-six holes at Augusta and

---

[3] See Appendix, "A Lesson from Bobby Jones."

Peachtree are his pieces of sculpture in earth, works of art passed down to stand as his gift to future generations of golfers. Considering his genius, they are comparable to the few paintings of Vermeer and the symphonies and concerti of Mozart.

It will add to our pleasure when we play the holes before us if we consider the effect they may have had on him during the important formative years when he first became aware of his gift. Do the memories of the rooms we lived in as children influence the design of the houses we build as adults? Most would agree, since what we choose to do as adults is strongly influenced, positively or negatively, by what we saw and heard when we were young. Did East Lake's par fives influence his design of thirteen and fifteen at Augusta? Perhaps the friendly approaches to many of the holes at East Lake inspired him to add challenge and drama at Augusta — by building those greens where they would be guarded by the tournament-wrecking water hazards the world knows so well. Maybe Tom Bendelow's sixteenth, "the Circus Ring," was in his mind when he laid out fifteen at Augusta. Even today the best of the best have to stop to think about the wind and their position in the tournament before choosing a club. Everyone who considers that shot learns what he wanted from golf, an exercise of mind and nerve as well as muscle.

Does every hole at East Lake contain some subtle key to his understanding of the game he mastered like none other? Ultimately, all golfers who learn the details and consider this issue will have to decide for themselves. One thing is certain, these are the only eighteen holes future generations can walk when they wish to experience the development of the genius of Bobby Jones.

Now, with the help of his friends, we'll play the course and pretend that Bobby, his father, and O.B. Keeler have come along to show us around and tell us their stories.

Before teeing off, some time may be spent on one of East Lake's practice greens. Up in front of the clubhouse, close to the entrance, the young Bobby Jones liked to practice putting in the moonlight, an unusual treat which he described in *Bobby Jones on Golf*:

> *I remember back in my high school days, I was living within the range of a good iron shot from the East Lake course, and on nights when the moon was out, I used to go over to the club and putt, with a friend and neighbor, on the practice green near the tenth tee. The moonlight, of course, revealed the hole, and it also made visible the more prominent slopes and irregularities — wormcasts and the like. In this half-revealing light, it was a source of wonderment to my friend and me that we invariably putted better than in broad daylight, especially*

when it came to holing out from distances up to eight or ten feet.

There must be something to be learned from that moonlight putting. I believe it to be this — the men who putt well on greens good and bad must have schooled themselves to see a putting green as we used to see it in the moonlight.

He quoted Alex Smith's response to why he never removed wormcasts from the path of the ball since the little obstructions might deflect the ball away from the hole: "Aye, and they might bounce it into the cup too."

Alex Smith, from Carnoustie, was the first head professional at East Lake and was a two-time U.S. Open champion (1906 and 1910). As club pro, he preceded Jimmy Maiden, Stewart Maiden (the model of the Jones swing), 1909 U.S. Open Champion George Sargent, and his son Harold Sargent, who became President of the PGA. The Director of Golf at the new East Lake Golf Club, Rick Burton, and his predessesor Jim Gerber, have impressive pedigrees.

ONE

Number one is a 424-yard par four which is played into the prevailing breeze. In *Down the Fairway*, Bobby discussed strategy on a golf course and illustrated the importance of thinking during a match by describing his play on East Lake's first hole during the 1927 Southern Open. He had been discussing how the decision to play a difficult recovery is affected by whether the issue is match or medal play:

> *Starting the third round of that competition, I pulled my drive to a peculiarly difficult situation behind some trees at the edge of the lake, which encroaches upon the left edge of the fairway some 240 yards from the tee. I found the ball lying well on the bank of the lake, with a decently large opening through the trees in the direction of the green. In an informal match some days previously I had driven to almost the same spot and had played through the trees to the green for my par 4. This was different. A championship was at stake in that tournament, at medal play. So I looked over the situation, concluded that I assuredly would not be as well off after a failure of the recovery shot — it almost certainly must have wound up in the lake, unless it came off — turned my back*

on the flag, and chipped modestly to a safe
place in the fairway. From there I had a com-
fortable shot to the green, and a 5; not so good
as a 4, certainly, but infinitely better for my
state of mind, as well as for the card, than a 6
or a 7 — or an 8.

Dr. Cyrus Strickler of Atlanta was one of the few
friends of Bobby's who was invited to play with him
at Augusta after the Masters every year during the
thirties and forties. Four foursomes were formed and
Bobby played in a different group every day.

He remembered when the man he knew only as a
great golfer became a friend. In 1924, Cy was eighteen
years old and was qualifying for the Georgia State
Amateur at the Capital City Club. He was one under
par when he walked onto the eighth tee, the water
hole on that course. He was surprised to see Bobby
Jones sitting on a bench beside the tee: "Everyone
knew Bob but I knew he didn't know who I was. I
tipped my cap to him on the way to the place I was to
tee up my ball. He said, 'Hello, Cy.' I was so flustered
that I topped that ball right into the lake."

Cy said that he only had one golf lesson in his life
and it was at East Lake by Stewart Maiden, the famous
Scot who was the model of Bobby's swing. "Several of
my golfing friends had told me for months that I stood
too far away from the ball. Since it felt right to me, I
kept standing in the same position, but when I went to

see Maiden I expected him to tell me to stand closer. He gave the lesson on the first tee rather than down in the practice area. I soon found out why. He was feeling the effects of some alcohol and was in an unusual expansive mood. While I hit ball after ball down the first fairway, he stood out in the driveway greeting all of the big shots who were driving in. He was stopping the cars and shaking their hands and chatting loudly while I worked away. It didn't seem that he was paying me the slightest attention. Finally, when I'd finished a third bag, I called over to him, 'What do you think?' He looked up from the driveway and yelled, 'Stand farther away from the ball.'"

Charlie Harrison remembers watching Bobby drive on the first hole right after World War II. "I was struck by how he positioned his club-head on the ground inside the ball. I thought he was going to use a practice swing since the toe of the club was an inch inside the ball. There was no practice swing, he quickly hit away. I don't know now whether he always did that or only did it late in his career."

During his record-setting round, on September 16, 1922, Bobby used a driver and hit a spade mashie[4] to twenty feet. He sank the putt for birdie three.

---

[4] Names of clubs in 1922: Driver–Driver; Brassie–two wood; Spoon–three wood; Baffey–four wood; cleek or driving iron–one iron; midiron–two iron; mid-mashie–three iron; mashie iron–four iron; mashie–five iron; spade mashie–six iron; mashie-niblick–seven iron; pitching niblick or lofting iron–eight iron; niblick–nine iron; putter–putter; jigger–an iron with a thin blade usually used for chipping, which had an angle of loft similar to a mashie.

In 1922, Bobby's clubs had hickory shafts. His woods were all wood, except for the leather grips and lead weights. Also, the pitching wedge and sand wedge did not exist in 1922. He called his driver *Jeannie Deans* and his putter *Calamity Jane*.

TWO

The second is a 192-yard par three played over a pond. Because of the steep slope between the green and the pond, when the pin is on the front, a shot hit at the hole risks bouncing back into the water or into a trap touching the front edge of the green. Like many old courses, the holes at East Lake are close to each other; a hard pull from the second tee can reach a group standing on the third. The closeness adds intimacy; it's easy to visit with your friends, and fun to watch them struggle.

In the summer of 1908, six-year-old Bobby Jones lived in a rented house just beyond today's second green, which was close by the thirteenth of Tom Bendelow's original course. The old thirteenth green was where the pond on the second hole is now.

In the *East Lake Country Club History*, Charlie Elliott described the Jones family's house in 1908. *Robert* is Colonel Robert P. Jones, Bobby's father.

> *This second summer has his family again moved to East Lake for the season, but instead of living with Mrs. Meadow, Robert rented a building on club property. It was located between the present No. 2 green and tennis court layout.*[5] *The ground story of this building was arranged to house livestock used to pull the East Lake fairway mowers and other*

[5] Today's parking lot is where the tennis courts were until 1994.

equipment and had been used for this purpose
before the house was renovated as a summer
residence. It was then, forever after, as long as
it stood, known as 'the Mule House.'

In those days the thirteenth hole was located near
the Mule House, and after following Maiden for a few
holes the young Jones would go home to the thirteenth
and spend hours pitching a capful of balls to the flagstick and putting them out.

"Through all my career," he once said, "I've never
been able to pitch a ball as accurately as I could pitch
it to the flagstick on that green."

Before leaving the second green, we might look
back across the tee toward the ninth tee. From 1908-
1913, this was the young Bobby's view of Tom
Bendelow's old number fourteen, a short uphill par
four which played across the "Spectacle" bunker, a
large trap shaped like a pair of eyeglasses, which was
in the woods between the tees of the modern second
and ninth holes.

In September of 1922, Bobby played the second at
150 yards, similar to the length from today's blue tees.
He hit another spade mashie and had only a three-foot
putt for a second birdie. He was two under par after
two holes.

THREE

Number three is now a 387-yard par four which requires an accurate drive to avoid large fairway bunkers between 200 and 250 yards. The greatest danger is the out-of-bounds fence and trees close to the right edge of the fairway, all the way to the green. On both the tee shot and the approach from the right, the overhanging limbs increase the danger of OB for those who always draw the ball. For this reason, the third is one of the few holes at East Lake where a slight fade is preferred. From the fairway, the two large traps guarding the right front of the green look like four; the golfer is encouraged to come in with another fade through the open door on the left.

A local expert on the history of the property, Tom Harding, knows that the third fairway crosses the site of the old Fayetteville Road, which ran from Decatur to the town of Fayetteville, south of Atlanta. Across the fence from the third fairway is an old-fashioned house with a surrounding porch, which is one house east of Third Avenue and sits slightly askew. That's because it was built in 1856 to face the Fayetteville Road, long before either Alston Drive or the golf course existed. That road ran in front of the present third green and occupied the space between the current fourth and eighth fairways. The large trees by the traps on the western side of the eighth fairway mark the site of the old road. From there, it continued along the little ridge between holes four and eight and left the current golf course to the west of the big oak tree guarding the fourth green. Today it's easy to visualize the old roadbed by standing on the eighth tee and looking toward the fairway traps on the left. After leaving the course, it's interesting to find the road outside the club property — it heads south to Fayetteville a few yards west of the intersection of Second Avenue and Glenwood. The northern remnant of the road leaves East Lake Drive south of its intersection with Oakview.

The man who built that house, which is now on Alston Drive, was Robert Alston. His farm, named *Meadow Nook*, was a 400 acre spread including Doolittle Creek, which feeds the lake today.

Tom tells an interesting story about Colonel Alston. During the Civil War, he rose from the rank of private to colonel in one year and became second in command of the Second Kentucky Cavalry. That unit, also known as *Morgan's Raiders*, was headquartered in the house from late in 1863 into the spring of 1864, when 2,000 troops from the Kentucky Cavalry camped out all over the farm, part of which is now the golf course. After the war, in 1878, Colonel Alston founded the *Atlanta Herald*, the newspaper which was the forerunner of today's *Constitution*, with the man who became the spokesman of the *New South*, Henry Grady. The new owners of the historic house, which is one of the oldest in Atlanta, Charles and Sylvia Harrison, have learned that Colonel Alston was killed in a gun-battle in downtown Atlanta by a man named Cox. Apparently the fatal confrontation occurred inside the old State House, which was then at the corner of Forsyth and Marietta Streets.

Today, if you shank your approach shot on number three over the fence out of bounds toward the Alston house, you can blame the ghosts of those cold Confederate soldiers who camped on this ground in the winter of 1863, one hundred and thirty-five years ago.

Seventy-six years ago, fifty-nine years after Morgan's Raiders, the young Bobby Jones was playing the third hole in what was to be the lowest round of his career. In 1922, from 320 yards, Bobby drove 290 yards and pitched with a mashie-niblick to four feet but missed the short putt — still two under par.

FOUR

As we walk onto the fourth tee it's interesting to look north beyond the intersection of Second Avenue and Alston Drive a few lots up on the left. That is where a stone house was where one of East Lake's famous sons, Charlie Yates, used to spend his summers. Charlie remembers climbing the fence when he was a boy to follow the man who later became his friend around the golf course. After a round, Bobby took Charlie and the other boys who followed him around into the clubhouse and bought them all a Coca-Cola, which Charlie loves to call "the elixir of Atlanta."

While walking down the fairway after hitting their drives, golfers who look to the left will be treated to a beautiful picture of the clubhouse in the distance, framed by two maples — it's one of the best sights on the property.

Certain members remember when the fourth was played with the sounds of a service heard through the loudspeaker of a church in the background.[6] Some said the praying helped, some said it hurt. East Lake was one of the few places in the world where you could go to church and play golf at the same time.

Today, the fourth is a straightaway 440-yard par four which plays north to south. But back in October of 1913, the last year of the Tom Bendelow course, it was the par four twelfth and played the other way, to the north. In *Down the Fairway*, Bobby said this was the site of "the greatest shot I ever saw."[7]

Vardon got the birdie at number twelve, but Ray, in getting his par four, produced this astonishing shot. His drive was the longest of

[6] The Ideal Spiritual Church of Deliverance, 341 Second Avenue (before 1994).

[7] Englishmen Harry Vardon and Ted Ray were the two greatest golfers of the day. They were touring the country and came to East Lake. Earlier in 1913 they had been tied and beaten in a playoff at the U.S. Open at Brookline by Francis Ouimet, the first American to win our Open.

the four, as usual, but right behind a tree. The tree was about forty feet in height with thick foliage, and the ball was no more than the tree's altitude in back of it, the tree exactly in line with the green. As Ray walked up to his ball, the more sophisticated members of the gallery were speculating as to whether he would essay to slice his shot around the obstacle to the green 170 yards away, or 'pull' around on the other side. As for me, I didn't see anything he could possibly do but accept the penalty of a stroke into the fairway. He was out of luck, I was sure.

Big Ted took one look at the ball and another at the green, a fair iron shot away, with the tree between. Then without hesitation he drew a mashie-niblick, and hit that ball harder, I believe, than I have ever seen a ball hit since, knocking it down as if he would drive it through to China. Up flew a divot the size of Ted's ample foot. Up also came the ball, buzzing like a partridge from the prodigious spin imparted by that tremendous wallop — almost straight up it got, cleared that tree by several yards, and sailed on at the height of an office building to drop on the green not far from the hole — the gallery was in paroxysms. I remember how men pounded each other on

*the back, and crowed and cackled and shouted
and clapped their hands. As for me, I didn't
really believe it. A sort of wonder persists in
my memory to this day. It was the greatest shot
I ever saw.*

Today, golfers playing this part of the course may
be treated to the beautiful sound of the call to prayer
by the muezzin at the mosque a block away from the
course, where the present Fayetteville Road heads
south from Glenwood Avenue.[8]

In 1922, the fourth was a short par five of 450
yards. Bobby's drive was long but ran into the rough
"at the elbow of the fairway." He then hit an iron to
twenty-five feet and took two putts for his third birdie
in four holes.

FIVE

In 1994, Rees Jones stretched what was a long
par four during the Ryder Cup back to the
length when Bobby played it. Today it is a 561-
yard par five which plays with the prevailing
wind from the west. If a golfer has already run into
trouble and is getting gloomy, the view down the fairway while walking to his ball should help. At any time
of year it is a spectacular sight to look all the way
down to the lake along this hole. The back nine, and

---

[8] The Atlanta Masjid of Al-Islam.

the hope of another bet in an hour, can be seen in the distance.

In 1919, professional "Long Jim" Barnes (no kin to Tommy) became the first Southern Open champion by beating seventeen-year-old Bobby Jones by one stroke. The pivotal hole was the 600-yard fifth where Barnes scored an eagle three, the only one ever shot on that hole in competition. The eagle three was not the conventional two wood shots and long putt. Bobby described the play in *Down the Fairway*: "He then pulled his drive far into the rough on the 600-yard fifth hole, pushed a brassie clear across the fairway into the rough on the other side, and then holed out a mashie shot of 150 yards for an eagle 3, while I was plugging along for a par 5." That Barnes went on to win the 1921 U.S. Open by nine shots, the largest winning margin in this century. Bobby finished fifth that year, tied with Alex Smith, the former East Lake professional.

The personality of Bobby Jones is illustrated by several stories. After he returned from World War II, he promised many good friends that he was going to design a new course in Atlanta, the course that became Peachtree Golf Club. He knew the job would demand an enormous amount of time. He kept procrastinating. Finally, one day on the fifth hole at East Lake, he had to wait to hit his approach while a slow foursome deliberately chipped and putted. He walked back and forth across the fairway, kicking the ground and getting upset. Finally, he'd had enough. Tommy Barnes remembers that he snatched his ball up off the fairway and stormed off the course, saying angrily: "Let's go build that new course." Everyone who knew him loved his warmth, his sense of humor, and his loyalty to his friends, regardless of their station in life, but they were also aware of his fierce intensity and impatience, especially with himself. He hated slow play in golf, and arrogance, insensitivity, and self-promotion in people.

Tommy was asked one time if he could recall Bobby ever saying anything about his record 63: "Bob never talked about his own game, he was that kind of person. He was always more interested in what you were doing."

The unwillingness to boast about his own accomplishments was a lifelong trait. Charlie Yates remembers Bobby's office in the C & S Bank Building in downtown Atlanta. No artifacts were there to glorify his career, no trophies, no plaques of appreciation, no photos with royalty and heads of state. Charlie says that only two things were present to indicate that the resident was a golfer. One was a sketch of the layout of the Old Course at St. Andrews. The other was a painting of a dilapidated golf bag stuffed with old clubs, inscribed with a poem by Grantland Rice:

For when the one great scorer
comes to write against your name,

He writes not that you won or lost,
but how you played the game.

Charlie will never forget the charming way that Bobby expressed criticism to his friends. After World War II, General Eisenhower and Bobby asked Charlie to become Southern Chairman of the U.S.O., a job which Bobby had to decline because of his poor health. One day he wanted his older friend's advice about an important letter to all the state chairmen. After reading it quietly and thoughtfully, he looked up at Charlie and smiled: "Charlie, it's great, just about right for you I'm sure. The only thing I can think to say is that it's a little bit flowery for me."

When Bobby shot his record 63 in September of 1922, the fifth was a 590-yard par five. He drove 310 yards and hit his brassie 260 yards to the edge of the green. O.B. Keeler wrote that he "chipped dead" for his fourth birdie, and he had only played five holes.

SIX

Number six is a picture-book 164-yard par three almost entirely surrounded by water. It usually plays into a cross wind which comes out of an oak tree guarding the approach on the left, a big obstacle which refuses to allow a fade to hold the green. A hard draw into the wind is preferred, and it must be hit perfectly as the only "bail-out" is a small area beyond the green. East Lake is waiting. A sad sight is an entire foursome, heads drooping, playing from the drop area. The sixth was on the 1992 list of the best eighteen holes in Georgia, selected by the Professional Golf Association of Georgia; and the Ryder Cup version was a lot easier than the new hole by Rees Jones.

Many members consider the view from the sixth tee and green their favorite, as the expanse of the lake and back of the clubhouse can best be appreciated from these spots. Others say these are good but not the best, which is coming up.

Mariana Goldsmith was on "the island hole" in 1920 when she saw a thunderstorm coming: "I left my clubs, ran around the green, dove into the lake, and swam back to the clubhouse."

During a round in the thirties, Bobby Jones announced to his foursome that he had finally figured out how to play number six. The friend on the tee said, "Thank God, I've never known what to do here. Quick, what is it?" Bobby gave his quizzical smile: "Use an old ball."

In the winter of 1991, Tommy hooked his tee shot into the big oak. It hit the biggest limb close to the trunk, skimmed out along it like a fast squirrel, took a big bounce off the cross tie by the lake, and dropped on the green. "Look at that. I've never seen that, as many times as I've played this hole. Something new always happens in golf."

Before leaving the sixth tee, we can let our minds go back to 1910 and look for old number ten. In those days, golfers finishing the front nine walked across the dam to the tenth tee, close to where we are now, and played due west along the fifth hole to a green which was in the center of the current fifth fairway about 200 yards from today's fifth green. A flat place in the rolling fairway marks the spot. Before 1914, from this old tenth tee, they could look north down the hill toward the lake to a green surrounded by water, which is our sixth green today. However, those hickory-shafted golfers were looking at the green of the par five sixteenth, which started far up the hill at the modern eighth tee and played down to the lake on the land between the current fifth and seventh holes. Bobby told Charlie Elliott that it was called "the Circus Ring," probably because of the appearance of the green surrounded by water.

In the 1940's and '50's, East Lake was one of the busiest country clubs in Atlanta. On summer afternoons, the beach at the edge of the lake was swarming with children and their parents swimming in the cool water. There was a lifeguard stand. As we stand on the sixth tee today, it's interesting to know what Charlie Harrison remembers. As a lifeguard, he was attentive to the swimmers, but the golfers playing number six were also directly in front of him. When their balls found the water, he carefully noted the location of each splash on a home-made diagram he kept in his lap. Later, he took out his canoe and looked for the balls.[9]

In 1922, Bobby hit a mashie to ten feet and took two putts for par three to stay four under par.

SEVEN

The seventh is a 394-yard par four which rises gently all the way, usually plays into the wind, and looks and behaves like it lives in Troon rather than Atlanta. With a long to mid iron, the approach, because of the wind, the narrow opening, and big bunkers, is one of the hardest shots on the course. However, an outstanding drive beyond the bunker is rewarded by leaving a short iron to the elevated green. The opening to the green looks flat and friendly from the fairway, but the slope to either side discards the short approach shot into one bunker or the other; it's hard to run-up onto this green.

In *Harvey Penick's Little Red Book,* a story is told which took place on the seventh:

Bobby Jones hit the best golf shot I ever saw in a tournament. I was playing in the group 150 yards behind him at East Lake in Atlanta at the Southern Open and had a clear view.

On the seventh hole there is a big canyon on

[9] Charlie Harrison became another well-known East Lake golfer. He won the Southern Amateur in 1955.

30

the right of the green with a grassy hollow at the bottom. The weather had been nasty, and suddenly hailstones as big as marbles began falling. The whole green was covered with hailstones. Jones had been down in the grassy hollow, but had pitched the ball just to the crown of the hill where he could hardly tell a golf ball from a hailstone. From there, he chipped the ball among the hailstones and it rolled right into the cup — for a par.

Jones had a way of doing whatever was necessary . . .

On the seventh tee we may sight up the hill to the right of today's fairway across the current fairway trap toward the bend in the eighth fairway. This was young Bobby's view of old number seventeen, a straight par four (before 1914).

During his record-setting 63 in 1922, Bobby bunkered his mashie second into the left front trap but blasted out to three feet with a niblick and sank the par putt — still four under.

EIGHT

The eighth is a 360-yard par four which should be played right to left from the tee to avoid the large fairway traps on the left. The expert golfer may try a bold drive over the traps, and if it comes off, the approach shot will be short. A strong fade means trouble as the ball may run off to the right behind two big white pines. One hundred yards from the green the fairway is crossed diagonally by a grassy depression which Dean Hudson, a deceased longtime member, said was a trench in the Civil War.[10]

Atlantan Richard Courts was a longtime friend and expert tennis player who exercised with Bobby during the winter before his assault on the Grand Slam in 1930. They went over to the stage of an abandoned theater downtown several times a week to play a badminton-like game with heavy rackets and a huge bird that Bobby had learned in California. He called it *Doug* after its inventor, Douglas Fairbanks. Both friends lost weight because of the regular exercise; the tennis player lost fifteen pounds but the golfer lost thirty-five. He may have had to work harder.

Richard Courts and his other friends always knew RTJ, Jr. as Bob. He said that he was *Little Bob* at first for contrast and later to compliment his father, who

---

[10] The depressions in the ground on the fourth and eighth holes were defensive lines, dug to protect the southern flank of encamped soldiers from attack along the Fayetteville Road.

was called *Big Bob* for the same two reasons. He never heard his friend called Bobby until he came back from a successful trip to Scotland:

> *Bob said: 'Richard, why don't you come with me? The people are delightful and the golf courses are the best and most difficult in the world.'*
>
> *I asked: 'You mean you're going all that way just to play golf?'*
>
> *When he was over there he won an important tournament and was awarded what he called later 'the most magnificent trophy I ever saw.' We read in the paper that after the tournament a big crowd formed around him for the presentation of this trophy. Bob told the crowd that he couldn't possibly take such a wonderful trophy away and that he would be honored to simply have his name inscribed at the bottom and know that it was safe in that delightful place.*
>
> *Well, those words touched every person in that crowd. When he finally had to leave they began shouting 'our Bobby' and 'wee Bobby.' After that, every time Bob set foot in Scotland or England he was a sensation. There was*

something about him that let them pretend he
was their own. He was unlike many Americans
they knew — there was fire but no arrogance
and no bragging.

Richard remembered walking the course at East
Lake one day with Bobby when the two got caught in
a severe thunderstorm [we think on the eighth hole]:
"We threw our bags away and ran but the lightning
was so close we couldn't go far. We looked down into
a gully hoping to hide [possibly the trench] but it was
full of water so we had to give up and lay face down
on open ground to wait for the storm to pass. It
seemed like an hour went by with our faces pressed
against that wet grass. We were scared to death."

Richard's first trip to East Lake to play golf was a
vivid memory as it was the first time he met RTJ, Jr.
He was standing with his host on the practice tee
watching a young man hit one beautiful arching shot
after another. He turned to his host: "I'm used to paying good money to see golf like that." His friend
replied: "Well, you're going to pay today; that's Little
Bob and he's going to be my partner. You're playing
with his father and Little Bob has just started to beat
Big Bob."

Colonel Jones joined Richard's first Board of
Directors at his new company, Atlantic Realty, and he
proved to be a wonderful colleague and friend. Once
the two men were visiting the Withams on West

Andrews Drive in Atlanta. They were gathered around a tub of potatoes boiling in resin out in the back yard when Colonel Jones burst into song. Richard remembered the details: "It happened to be the week that the Metropolitan Opera was in town. Big Bob started singing 'Ole Man River' in his wonderful baritone — he knew every word of every verse. It was a wonderful sound. About halfway through, a messenger arrived with a note from Dr. Phinizy Calhoun's house next door. They wanted to know which opera star was singing, and could they come over."

In 1922, the eighth was either a par three or a par four, depending on the time of year. The tee was close to today's position, and the par three winter green was at the top of the hill to the right of the modern fairway, which was also the site of Tom Bendelow's seventeenth green (1908-1913). The Donald Ross summer green for number eight was where the green is today, and in hot-weather months the eighth was usually played as a par four.

Before leaving the tee on number eight, we may remember that it was the tee for the sixteenth hole before 1914 (the Circus Ring). As we imagine we are on that old tee, we can look east through the pine trees down toward the lake and see the current sixth green in the distance down the old fairway between holes five and seven. If no one else is around we might take a few extra minutes to play the Circus Ring. Today, an excellent drive will carry the trees at the top of the old fairway, which would be a 250-yard drive just beyond the top of the hill. From there, we will see the current sixth green surrounded by water. When Bobby was a boy, the members must have called the hole the Circus Ring because of the way the green looked from the top of the hill — or maybe they were thinking that trying to hit that green from that distance was as risky as trying the flying trapeze without a net.

If the wind was out of the west, perhaps the long hitters could take advantage of a downhill roll on hard ground and hit the ball more than 300 yards. Since the old sixteenth measured 535 yards, they would still have well over 200 yards to reach the small green, with water front and back. Did eleven-year-old Bobby Jones usually reach it in three? No one knows, but we can count on one thing—since he played that par five many times before age eleven, the details were fixed in his mind.

Since the drive was along level ground to the top of a hill, with green and water in the distance below, it's interesting to imagine that the old hole at East Lake may have been the inspiration for the fifteenth at Augusta National. If it was, Bobby must have loved the chance to improve on the Circus Ring by making the hole at Augusta shorter and reachable in two by the expert golfer who needs an eagle. Also, on the second hole at Peachtree, the top golfer's mind turns to the same decision—"should I go for it or lay up?" Is there a link back to East Lake in both of those famous golf courses? Perhaps.

Back to the eighth, which was a 230-yard par three when played by Bobby during his record-setting 63 in 1922. O.B. Keeler wrote that he missed the green with a long iron but hit a niblick to eight feet and sank the putt to save par and remain at four under.

NINE

The wonderful ninth, a 551-yard par five, requires a long draw off the tee. Before the hill was removed in 1994, a well-hit drive by an average golfer would run down close to the lake, and good golfers could try for the green on their second shots. Today, however, most are faced with a long carry over water, which may be from a downhill lie, a nerve-racking shot. When going for the green from across the lake, the shot played to the left may find the fairway bunker. From there, a fifty-yard sand shot is required, which will need to be hit with enough height to allow it to stop within the narrow target. That is another one of the hardest shots on the course.

A beautiful view of the lake and clubhouse slowly develops as we leave the ninth tee. At this place, and at many others, the golfer seems to be walking in the park of an old English estate. The clubhouse, like the manor house, is central and dominant, and can be reached quickly from anywhere on the course, a comforting safety feature in threatening weather.

Bobby's father, Colonel Jones, is a legend at East Lake and many of his colorful quotes have survived. Once, on the ninth, he hit a high sweeping slice that started left, crossed the entire fairway and plunged into the woods on the right. The Colonel shouted after it: "That's it, go on in there, you sightseeing sonofabitch."

Charlie Yates wrote a delightful afterword in Bobby's little book *The Basic Golf Swing*, which contains some wonderful stories about the Colonel.

One day [we think on the ninth tee], he topped a tee shot that went about a hundred and twenty-five yards. He backed away and took a practice swing. Then he turned to his son and said: 'What's wrong with that swing?'

Bob replied, 'Nothing, Dad. Why don't you try it sometime?'

However, the all-time best story about the Colonel took place one afternoon in the early days of the Masters when Cliff Roberts, finding himself short of a Rules Committeeman, asked the Colonel to go out to the most sensitive spot on the course, the twelfth hole. The Colonel was standing behind the eleventh green when he suddenly heard the call for a Rules Committeeman to come to the twelfth green. The Colonel went there and saw a player standing on the bank wanting to know if he was outside the hazard and, therefore, entitled to a free lift. He asked the Colonel if the embedded ball rule was in effect, and the Colonel had not the slightest idea about this rule.

The Colonel countered: 'Let me ask you a question, son. How do you stand with par?' The player replied: 'Well, sir, today I am seven over and, for the tournament, twenty-three over.' The Colonel responded: 'Hell, son, I don't give a damn what you do with it — put the sonofabitch on the green for all I care!'

Back to the ninth at East Lake: During the Ryder Cup Matches in 1963 a member recalled watching Julius Boros play his second from the Bermuda rough down near the lake on the right side: "He took a full swing with a wood, but both the ball and the club stayed in the rough. That grass pulled the club right out of his hands."

On October 9, 1963, in an article in *The Atlanta Journal*, Ed Miles told an interesting story from a practice round for the Ryder Cup.

Palmer and his playing crew of Lema, Casper,

and Pott were laughing at their play of the ninth hole, a particularly treacherous link of the East Lake trail.

'We did it up proper,' said Johnny Pott, who just the day before had made the only eagle three yet recorded on the ninth hole. 'Lema had a five, I had a six, Arnie had a seven and Casper had an eight.' Casper, standing by, added with a chuckle: 'And I had to drop a six-foot putt for that eight.' It seems the jovial roly-poly Californian had water trouble, followed by a shot wheeled clear over into the parking lot.

Since a par five had been on this site since 1908, it is unlikely that Pott's eagle three in 1963 was the first. However, the changes for the Ryder Cup had only recently been completed and Potts' three was the first of many on that version. Until 1994, the parking lot was where the practice tee is today.

Late one day in the mid fifties, Tommy Barnes hit a two iron second shot from a flat lie close to the lake. Since a foursome was still on the green, Tommy intended to lay it up short for an easy pitch. He didn't count on hitting the best long iron of his life. The ball hit twenty yards in front, bounded onto the green, rolled by the man putting, and wound up a foot from the hole. His most embarrassing eagle gave him a 29 for the front nine. Unfortunately, he couldn't finish the round that day — it was too dark.

On April 26, 1989, at age seventy-three, Tommy Barnes completed his 62, the course record on the Ryder Cup course, by scoring his seventh birdie of the day on number nine, to go with two eagles and one bogie. Ten under par on a full-length course had never been done before by a man as old as seventy-three; and it has not been done since.

Over the years, other East Lake golfers have been touched by magic and scored outstanding rounds. Tommy remembers rounds in the low 60's by his son, Tommy Jr., and Charlie Harrison remembers a day in April, 1964 when the unexpected happened to him.

Charlie had talked his friend Allen Hardin into playing nine holes, but he changed his plan when his putt on the ninth spun out to give him an even 30 for the front nine. He turned to his friend, "Allen, I've got to keep going." He shot a 33 on the back to finish with 63.[11]

Tom Bendelow's eighteenth green was where the ninth is today, and the old eighteenth tee before 1914 was close to the modern ladies' tee. That old finishing par five was pretty much the same as the modern ninth. In 1913 eleven-year-old Bobby Jones sank a four foot putt there to score 80 for the first time. The

---

[11] Like any golfer who shoots any score at any time, these low 60 shooters remember where they could have saved at least two more strokes. Apparently, in golf even perfection leaves something to be desired.

event is described by O.B. Keeler in *The Bobby Jones Story*:

> *On this summer day, he was playing with Perry [Adair] as usual, but for once — and for the first time — he wasn't paying any attention to what Perry was doing. He was scoring better than he ever had scored before and he had no room in his mind for anything else. At the last green, faced with a four-foot putt for an even 80, he must have wondered why his skinny little chest was so tight and why his hands were trembling as he stood up to that putt, not to beat Perry but just to score an 80. Down went the putt and on the card went the 80, with the signature of Perry Adair on the attested line.*
>
> *And away across the golf course went Bobby Jones, setting off at a brisk trot to find his dad. He found Big Bob at the fourteenth green [between the present ninth tee and eighth green], and he walked solemnly up to him and held out the card — without a word — his hand still trembling. Big Bob took the card and looked at it. Then he looked at Bobby. Then he put his arms around him and hugged him hard. And so before he was a dozen years old, Bobby Jones had discovered a new adversary in golf,*

*the Great Opponent whose tangible form is
only a card and a pencil. He had played his
first round against the toughest foeman of
them all — Old Man Par.*

In 1925, outside of the old pro-shop close to the
ninth green, twelve-year-old Charlie Yates walked up
to his famous older friend, who had just been beaten
in the U.S. Open.

Charlie said, "I'm sorry you lost."

Bobby Jones looked down kindly and replied,
"Thank you, son. . . . You never know who your
friends are until you lose."

In 1922, O.B. Keeler reported that Bobby hit a
"fair drive to a heavy lie, a brassie short of the green,
and niblick to eight feet." He sank the putt for birdie
four to move to five under par. In nine holes, *Jeannie
Deans* found the fairway five of seven tries; the irons
reached in regulation on seven of nine; and *Calamity
Jane* was used twelve times. He had six one-putt
greens and turned in 31.

TEN

While we enjoy a needed break for iced tea in summer or hot chocolate in winter, a beautiful hole is waiting. The 516-yard uphill par five tenth begins the back nine in style. It requires a drive over the lake which will roll very little because of the rising fairway. For a top player who wants a birdie, both power and accuracy are required to stay out of the greenside bunkers and get home in two. He may *get* home with a long iron or wood, but *staying* home is another matter, as a ball hit from that distance may run off the back of the green.

As we play the tenth it's interesting to imagine that it's early summer in 1913 when a similar hole was the par four second. If it's close to 2 p.m., we can probably hear *the Suburban Express* pulling up at the end of the streetcar line close to the entrance of the club. The regular streetcar ride from Atlanta to East Lake took thirty minutes and made many stops. In addition, for packages and small freight there was one nonstop car every day called the Suburban Express, which left downtown at the corner of Alabama and Pryor Streets. It rushed out to East Lake with medicine or other supplies that had been ordered by phone or put on the car by husbands working downtown.

Those houses across the fence on Alston Drive are filled with families who have just arrived by moving

van from Atlanta for their vacations. A man is standing in front of the stucco bungalow, next to the corner lot on East Lake Drive. That's Dr. Stirling, an
ENT specialist who has just arrived with his three
daughters, Janet, Alexa, and Nora. Alexa will become
the first East Lake golfer to win a national championship. She will win three consecutive U.S. Women's
Amateur titles, in 1916, 1919, and 1920. (There was
no contest in 1917 and 1918 because of the war.)
Later she will move to Ottawa, become Alexa Fraser,
win the Canadian Ladies' Championship, and be
recognized as one of the best golfers in Canadian history.[12]

East of the Stirling house the ground sloped
down to "the frog pond" at the bottom of the hill
(the brick house next to the Stirling's, the park, and
playground were not present in 1913). During the
summer, the Goldsmith family lived in a brown shin-
gled house which stood on the corner of Alston Drive
and Daniel Avenue. If we had a time machine and
could travel back to 1913, we would see their nine-
year-old girl, Mariana, dressed for swimming and
standing by the fence, waiting for us to hit our drives.
As soon as we finish she'll sneak under the fence,
dash across the fairway, and dive into the lake to
start her perfect summer. In 1917, Mariana was the
person who first raised the flag in front of the new

---

[12] When Alexa left East Lake for Canada she told her friend Mariana Goldsmith: "One
thing I'm not going to do is play golf. My father made me play, but I never really
wanted to"–so much for denial of world-class talent.

clubhouse at East Lake.

The 1917 clubhouse was destroyed by fire in 1925, but it was re-created with its exposed Tudor beams in 1995. The new Bobby Jones Room and Great Hall reflect the 1927 style of architect Philip Trammell Shutze, who changed the dark wood panelling he had used in 1917 into his own lighter neoclassical style. During the renovation in 1995, these two masterpieces were restored to his exact specifications.

As we cross the lake and start up the hill we can look through the small park to an old-fashioned small red brick house which faces the park four lots in from Alston on Daniel Avenue. That was Mary Bell Meadow's boarding house. In 1907, this was where Colonel Jones first brought his five-year-old son and the rest of the family to escape the heat of the city. East Lake was then the only significant lake within an easy drive of Atlanta. Bobby's first swings were taken on a makeshift course with a hole along Alston Drive. He didn't have a hole-in-one until 1927, but he liked to point to that ditch and say that he had several one-shot holes before he was six years old.

Mariana remembers that everyone planning to eat with Mrs. Meadow would respond to the wonderful announcement of mealtime. Wiley, Mrs. Meadow's butler, used a megaphone to call across the golf course: "Supper is all ready."

Edna Raine Wardlaw, who is a lifelong Atlantan, used to visit her grandmother at East Lake, Mrs. John

A. Miller. Her house was next door to the Goldsmith's on the west side of Daniel Avenue, across the street from Mrs. Meadow's boarding house, where the park is today. As a seven- or eight-year-old child, she was told by her parents to "never go back across the creek because that's where the gypsies are." Edna says that naturally she and her friends became curious, and one day went across the creek to "spy" on the gypsy camp, which was where Green Street borders the small park. Edna remembers the scent of a bar of soap she found near the camp. It wasn't like anything she had smelled before. "I could remember that smell for many years."

Edna also remembers sleeping on the screened porch as a nine- or ten-year-old girl, in 1916 or 1917, while her parents and all of their friends were at the Saturday night dance across the street at the club. "The music from the orchestra coming across the lake was exciting, and I remember thinking how romantic it must have been, with all the men breaking in on my mother, asking her to dance."

Edna's husband, William C. Wardlaw, Jr., was a longtime member of Peachtree Golf Club, and was a benefactor to the city, especially to his, and Bobby's college, Georgia Tech.

The former house of another famous East Lake golfer, Watts Gunn, is nearby. The lovely two-story white-frame house still sits just off the tenth green, now almost hidden by huge magnolias. Bobby and

Watts were opponents in the final of the U.S. Amateur at Oakmont in 1925. It was, and still is, the only time two members of the same club have faced each other in the final of that tournament. On the first tee at Oakmont, Watts turned to Bobby and asked: "Are you going to give me my usual four strokes?" He said later that Bobby smiled and said, "I'm going to give you hell today." Watts remembered: "He wasn't kidding — that's exactly what he did."

Actually, Watts was a sensation at Oakmont. He electrified the large gallery all week with his marvelous play and Southern charm. The final match turned on the famous "Ghost Hole," the twelfth. Bobby wrote in *Down the Fairway*: "And my third shot (the hole is of 600 yards) was bunkered at the green, and Watts' was well on, for a sure par 5. When I went down into that bunker I was morally certain of one thing. If Watts took that hole from me I'd never catch him. He was playing the most ferocious brand of inspirational golf I had ever seen; he was 2 under par now, and he was about to take another hole from me." Bobby got up and down with a ten-foot putt for a half, reeled off a "hot run," and finally "settled matters" in the afternoon round.

Watts Gunn, like the other excellent golfers at East Lake in the 1920's and '30's, was more than that, he was an interesting character and a good friend. Tommy loves to tell about his gamesmanship during a match:

*I remember once when I had him down two or
three holes in a match and I was full of confidence, really hitting the ball. Watts was struggling, but he never stopped thinking. After hitting our balls on number six, while walking off
the tee, he turned to me and said, 'Tommy, I
didn't know you had changed your grip.' That
made me wonder about my grip, which of
course I hadn't changed at all. After that I got
to thinking that maybe I had, so I must have
done something different from then on in. I got
beat.*

*At another time, Watts said, late in the day,
'Well, I see we're in the shank of the evening,'
just to get the awful thought in my head.*

Watts was also famous for his favorite golfing
advice, "Keep your head down and your tail up," and
for his favorite exclamation, "Jeepers-Creepers!"

In 1993, Watts was taken on a ride around East
Lake, which he hadn't seen for years. Cartpaths and
golf carts were all over the place. Watts said, "East
Lake, I can't believe it; no caddies."

Over the years, East Lake has been used as a qualifying site for major tournaments many times, especially the U.S. Amateur. Once in the late fifties or early
sixties, Charlie Harrison and Tommy Barnes tried to
qualify for the Amateur together. Charlie remembers

that Tommy had an excellent first 27 holes. "He probably could have bogied every hole on the back and still
qualified." Nonetheless, like every golfer, a good per-
formance only whetted his appetite for more, and this
story illustrates that point.

> *Until about ten years ago, there was a large
> oak tree on the right side of the tenth fairway.
> Since there were no bunkers on the left and the
> fairway tilted that way from the center, a play-
> er would risk OB with a drive to the center of
> the fairway out of the way of the tree. Almost
> always, top players went a little to the right
> and had to deal with the big tree. Well, on his
> second shot on number ten, Tommy hit a hard
> low fade, just like he wanted to, but as so often
> happens, it hit directly on the last branch and
> dropped straight down. Tommy took his iron,
> walked angrily up to that branch, and swung
> like he was going to chop it off. Instead, he lost
> his balance and cracked himself hard on the
> right ankle with the blade. He could hardly
> walk the rest of the back nine that day, he had
> hurt himself so badly.*

Many years later, Tommy got his revenge. He was
in exactly the same situation, behind the same tree. A
playing partner laughed and challenged him by saying
sarcastically to the other members of the foursome,

"Well, let's see what the great Tommy Barnes does now." A few seconds later, Tommy sliced his iron around the tree, and the ball bounded up onto the green and jumped into the hole for eagle two . . . Tommy winked at his friends and smiled, "There's nothing to that shot."

In 1922, number ten was a par four of 425 yards. O.B. Keeler wrote: "Bobby drove far up the hill and hit a mashie to ten feet. The putt hit the back of the cup but hopped out and he settled for par four."

ELEVEN

This is a 192-yard par three which is played slightly uphill. When the pin is on the left, the bold shot risks being discarded down a hill behind a giant oak, into the oblivion of a bogey, or worse.

From the member's tees, Tommy once pushed a seven iron into the right bunker. He was disgusted with himself: "If a man can't hit a green with a seven iron, he ought to give up the game." Despite a back brace, he had even par 72 that day, which was two weeks short of his seventy-seventh birthday. Tommy Barnes must be one of the few men alive who has a bad day when he shoots his age.

From the back tees in the sixties, the hole seemed to curve around a tree on the right. When Arnold

Palmer first looked at the eleventh during a practice round for the 1963 Ryder Cup, he turned to a friend: "I've never seen a dog-leg par three before."

Charlie Yates remembers playing with Bobby one time on the par three eighth hole on the other course at East Lake, old East Lake # 2, which was close to the length from the blue tees of today's eleventh. Charlie did what all of us have done when we were young and strong and found ourselves playing with an older man we wanted to impress, such as a father or other idol. It seems that Bobby, the idol in this case, had just hit what was for him an ordinary shot, a five iron 160 yards to the center of the green. In this situation, the young man invariably wants to impress the older one by showing off his strength and skill. After seeing what Bobby had used, Charlie took out his seven iron, hooded the club for extra distance and swung harder than usual, hoping to hit a big hook to the green. The shot came off and the ball wound up on the green. Charlie, like each of us, waited for the expected, "Great shot, how wonderful it must be to be so bold and strong." Bobby just looked at him and dead-panned, "Charlie, don't you have any club in your bag other than that seven iron?" Charlie was properly deflated; no praise came out, only criticism for show-ing off.

Before eleven was changed for the Ryder Cup, the hole was shorter and the green was closer to Alston Drive. One day in the fifties, Ed Garner pulled his shot over into the road. The ball hit a car coming west toward the tee, bounced high into the air, and fell onto the green four feet from the hole. The driver stopped, got out and waved his hat. Ed sank the putt and recorded the most unusual birdie ever made at East Lake.

In 1922, when Bobby shot his record 63, the eleventh measured 175 yards. O.B. Keeler wrote that he hit his jigger to twenty feet and took two putts for par three.[13]

TWELVE

In 1994, Rees Jones moved the Ryder Cup green to the left to allow more room for number ten and built a classic Ross green with sloping shoulders and a huge front bunker touching the green. There is drama at the end of this peaceful-looking 391-yard downhill par four.

The twelfth tee is a beautiful spot as golfers turn to the west and get their first look at Atlanta's skyline. But it's only a peek; the real show is ahead. From here, a flicker of gold may be visible in the top of the trees; it is the sun's reflection off the dome of the State Capitol, six miles away.

In 1990, after hitting his tee shot well over the old

---

[13] In June of 1995, from 165 yards, young professional Paul Weir took his first swing ever with a hickory shafted club, a jigger similar to the one Bobby used in 1922. He knocked it well over the green. "I can't believe it," he said. "What a sweet club."

fairway trap 200 yards from the white tees, Tommy was asked if Bobby Jones could have done it from the blue tees, fifty yards behind. "Easy, Bob Jones could hit a golf ball as far as he needed to. But I never heard him say that he'd hit it just right. After a drive of 250 yards, I'd say: 'Great drive, Bob.' All he'd say was, 'a little on the heel' or, 'a little on the toe.' He was never satisfied with his own game."

Bobby's drive on number twelve in 1922 was followed by a mashie-niblick to eight feet from the cup. He sank the putt for birdie three and moved to six under par. At this point, he may have thought that if he could stay out of trouble on the remaining six holes, he would equal his own course record of 66, which he had set two years before at age eighteen, and tied four times since.

In 1922, despite his young age, Bobby Jones was familiar with the experience of setting course records. He had first set the record at East Lake at age thirteen, with a score of 77. Mr. D.E. Root, the owner of the record before Bobby, didn't have it long, since his record 78 in 1915 came only five days before Bobby's 77. Bobby then broke his own record with a 74 at age fourteen, set it again with a 70 at sixteen, then broke it twice at seventeen with rounds of 69 and 68. Then came the 66 at eighteen. Now here he was again, knocking on the door for the seventh time, and he was still only twenty years old.

Bobby was almost killed one time by lightning on

the twelfth green. He was putting out on that green in the summer of 1930, after the first three legs of the Grand Slam, when a bolt of lightning struck the ground only 40 yards away. After another one struck the thirteenth tee, Bobby and his group began running toward the clubhouse. Finally, in another near disaster, a bolt struck the large double chimney just before they reached cover. The lightning strike threw bricks 100 yards, and one barely missed doing serious damage — when Bobby got inside, his shirt had been torn and a six inch cut opened on his shoulder by falling debris.

THIRTEEN

The thirteenth is a 400-yard par four which winds back and forth up a gentle hill and, like number seven, looks more like Scotland than Atlanta. It is an unforgiving test that throws the fading tee shot away into the adjoining fairway, hopeless behind huge oaks. The hole asks for either a bold drive close to the trees on the left, over the fairway traps, or a long draw, the perfect shot only masters can pull off. This one is mean all the way home, for on the approach from the right all the golfer sees from the fairway are deep traps guarding the green, large and gaping. Because of the following breeze, the strong shot well over the bunkers risks bouncing through the green and off the course. Most members wind up short and pitch from the front.

Ed Garner is the only member of East Lake who can report what the young Jack Nicklaus did when he played thirteen. When he visited in the early sixties, Jack drove into a fairway trap which used to be on the right, 250 yards from the tee, then hit an eight iron to the green and sank the birdie putt.

Over the years, Bobby Jones made many birdies on the thirteenth, and one stands out in the memory of Charlie Harrison. It seems that in 1945, Charlie and his friend and relative, Tom Cousins, were spending a perfect summer day for young Georgia teenagers — a little life-guarding and a little swimming. Somehow the word got to Charlie that Bobby Jones was playing the back nine, and he called to his friend, "Come on Tom, we're going to see the best golfer in the world."

We rushed out to my 1932 Pontiac and drove out to behind the thirteenth green. We got there just as Bobby Jones was walking up to his drive and getting ready to hit his approach. Now in those days, there was a big tree guarding the left side of the green, and since Bobby's drive was to the left, the shot required a hook around that tree from the fairway. I remember the shot. There was no practice swing — instead he swung and hit the perfect shot —

the ball hooked just like it needed to and ended up a foot from the hole. I turned to Tom, 'See, he does it every time.'

No one can remember Bobby Jones taking practice swings, whether over the ball or at other times. He was always serious about the game at hand and hated having his concentration broken. A short passage in *Bobby Jones on Golf* speaks to both points.

The ethics of the game allow each person a reasonable opportunity to play each shot carefully, but they demand also that the player step up promptly to do his bit without unnecessary delay.

The habitual practice swingers, and there are numbers of them, have an uncanny talent for taking their swings at precisely the wrong times. Everyone has had the experience and knows how annoying it is hearing the swish of a club behind him just as he is in the midst of his swing. He has to be very fond of the culprit to restrain a desire to bash him on the head with a club, even when he knows that the guilt is only of thoughtlessness.

For "Hardy" in *The Legend of Bagger Vance*, the thirteenth at East Lake was the turning point in the match, and in his life. As he stood over his 1931 Spalding Dot, Mike said, "Hold nothing back."

During his record 63 in 1922, Bobby Jones drove 260 yards uphill, hit a spade mashie to twenty feet, and took two putts for par four, to stay at six under par.

FOURTEEN

On the tee of the fourteenth, a 442-yard par four, the host is torn between telling his guest "don't hook the ball into jail on the left" and remaining silent with a supportive and hopeful look. If the unsuspecting finds the low ground in the woods to the left, he may not be able to beat a six. The hole is so long that a four is a triumph. Fourteen feels like Muirfield — it's beautiful and elegant and usually plays into the wind. When the pin is back left, the long ridge by Rees Jones will cause the short approach to run away to the right, and the bold shot may disappear over the steep hill toward the seventeenth fairway.

One day in 1993, after Dick Boyens had hit his approach on the fourteenth, he noticed something moving on the green. When he got closer, he was amazed to find a big catfish frantically flopping around. He knew it couldn't have "walked" all the way across the seventeenth fairway up the hill to that spot. A man who had been mowing nearby told him what had happened: "A few minutes ago an osprey grabbed it out of the lake and flew over the green but couldn't hold on. That fish dropped right out of the sky. It's the damnedest thing I ever saw."

Everyone who played at East Lake before the renovation in 1994 remembers the special quality of the bunkers. The sand was always thin and special care needed to be taken to avoid sculling the ball. In 1935, in what O.B. Keeler called "the greatest match I ever witnessed," Joyce Wethered, the great English woman champion, was paired with Charlie Yates against Bobby Jones and fifteen-year-old Dorothy Kirby, who was destined to win the U.S. Women's Amateur. In *Bobby Jones on Golf*, Bobby wrote: "The first requisite of a truly sound swing is simplicity. In this respect, I think that the late Horton Smith and Lady Heathcoat-Amory, who as Miss Joyce Wethered played superb golf in my day, excel any golfers I have seen . . . I have found many to agree with me that Miss Wethered's swing was the most perfect in the world . . . ."

One of the bunkers on fourteen played a crucial role in the match.

Miss Wethered's driving was simply tremendous. The wind was coming up, and when facing it she was hitting a low, raking drive of great carry and astonishing run. And at the fourteenth, a hole of 448 yards, there was, for the moment, a half-gale coming out of the west, straight in her face. And there — well, Bobby and Charlie Yates struck off two of their best, and Miss Wethered's ball was well in front.

Against the sweeping wind, Miss Wethered was flag-high with her second shot, the ball curling off to the left into a bunker. And here ensued the most whimsical play of the afternoon.

Miss Wethered, of course, was unfamiliar with East Lake bunkers in summer, or at any other time. This was her first recovery off what looked to her as if it might be sand. She essayed a good, substantial half-blast with the niblick, and the blade, ricocheting from the sun-baked surface under a thin layer of sand, clipped the ball fairly in the back and sent it flying 50 yards over the green and the gallery, to the frank amazement of the latter and no less of Miss Wethered herself.

But she trotted down into a little valley, found the ball in a difficult place, pitched back beautifully, almost hitting the flag — and holed a 20

foot putt for a five, to be a stroke above par,
while Bobby won the hole with a four.

In his record-setting round, Bobby played the four-teenth as a 465-yard par five. He drove 300 yards and hit a mashie short of the green. The pin was near the front and "a wee pitch failed to stop promptly and ran fifteen feet past the pin." He took two putts for a disappointing par five and remained at six under par.

After leaving the green on fourteen, we walk today through a thick stand of mature white pines ("the Black Forest") toward the fifteenth tee. Between 1908 and 1913, we would be walking the wrong way on the sixth hole, a short par four, which started near the modern fifteenth tee and ended close to where the twelfth green is today.

FIFTEEN

The fifteenth is a 495-yard uphill left-to-right par five with large new bunkers on the right which are perfectly positioned to catch either the drive or fairway wood second shot because of the intentional fade, which the hole seems to want, and the right sloping fairway.

The thick woods to the right of the fairway give the best cover for small animals that exists on the golf course. For this reason, the red-tailed hawk may show himself here. It's always wise to check the branches; he may be watching.

In the *East Lake Country Club History*, Charlie Elliott told a classic story about Bobby's father, which had its climax on the fifteenth:

Colonel Bob loved a good story on himself, whether he or someone else was telling it, and one of those he enjoyed most was about what he called his 'most unusual tournament.'

This was an intra-club tournament held between the golfers of East Lake and those of another club in a town near Atlanta. The other club contained a golfer who was every bit as proficient in the use of profanity as the Colonel, so the tournament committee arranged to pair these two against one another in the same foursome. It was agreed among the intra-club committeemen that both the Colonel and his opponent would be told the same story — that he was playing against a preacher and to keep from embarrassing his club, it would be necessary to watch his language during the round.

Everyone who was in on the joke declared that it was probably the most hilarious round of golf ever played. When one of the contestants

*missed a shot — which was often — instead of
going into his usual verbal barrage which had
to do with the slings and arrows of outrageous
fortune, he would turn red in the face, control-
ling his temper with obvious effort. This went
on for fourteen holes, with the other members
of the foursome and the gallery scarcely able to
contain their hilarity.*

*On the 15th hole, the Colonel's opponent
missed a short putt. As he stooped over to pick
up his ball on the edge of the cup, he said
under his breath, 'goddamnedsonofabitch!'
The foursome froze for an instant and Colonel
Bob, only a step away, reached over and
caught the man by the arm.*

'What did you say?' he asked.

*'Why it was nothing — nothing,' the golfer
stammered.*

*The Colonel was persistent. 'What did you
say?' he demanded.*

*His opponent faced him, red to the tips of his
ears. 'Look, preacher,' he apologized, 'I could-
n't help it. It just slipped out. I'm sorry.'*

'Preacher?' Colonel Bob roared. 'Who's a preacher?'

'They told me you were,' the man mumbled, and the two studied one another, the light beginning to dawn.

Those who followed the match later declared that the air was blue from that point on to the clubhouse.

On the way to our second shots on fifteen, we cross the fairway of the old ninth hole of the Tom Bendelow course (1908-1913), which was a dogleg par four. The tee was at the top of the hill between the current fifteenth and fourteenth fairways east of the Black Forest. In those days the landing area was where the woods are today, between fifteen and sixteen. From age six to eleven, Bobby played that course and would have hit his drive over our heads as we walk along today's fifteenth fairway. The second shot was played across the end of the sixteenth fairway to a green between the current sixteenth green and the dam of the lake.

On Saturday June 3, 1995, a few members played the new back nine for the first time to help the new caddie training program. On fifteen, a visitor from Virginia, Cameron Stone, chipped in from fifty yards for an eagle three. Thirty seconds later, J.D. Ostrow, a young friend of Jim Gerber's from Maidstone on Long Island, did exactly the same thing. Taken together, it was the only "double eagle" ever recorded on fifteen. In the winter, the hole that Bobby played after 1913 was almost straight. Roger Cordes remembers that RTJ, Jr. liked to hit a long draw from the winter tee over the trees on the right which would climb the hill when it landed. Playing fifteen at 505 yards in 1922, Bobby drove 260 yards and hit a brassie uphill to the edge of the green. He took two putts from thirty feet for birdie four and was finally at seven under with three holes to go, a record-setting pace.

SIXTEEN

In 1994 Rees Jones transformed the sixteenth from the gentle short par five it had been into a severe test. At 481 yards, this par four into the wind is tougher than fourteen, a worthy challenge for the best golfers, and a very hard birdie so close to the end.

Years ago, the fairway on sixteen was bordered by a series of pot bunkers. Charlie Yates remembers that during a round with Pierce Harris, a famous Atlanta minister, Colonel Jones got in one bunker after another. The Colonel had controlled his language all the way around, but with the frustration building after every flub, out came a stream of cursing. Finally, with everyone on the green, Bobby sank a birdie putt and Charlie and the minister were closed out. Walking toward the seventeenth tee, Mr. Harris turned to his partner and said in a voice that was loud enough to be heard by the Colonel and his son: "Charlie, we should have known that we could not compete today against such a combination of proficiency and profanity."

Back to 1935 and the match with Joyce Wethered, as told by O.B. Keeler:

> Going down the fairway toward the sixteenth green, I was walking momentarily with Miss Wethered, and, naturally, I was complimenting her on her brilliant play. She smiled and then became suddenly grave. 'I had to play well here', she said simply, 'Bobby arranged the match, you know. And he's said and written so many kind things about my game. And then he was ill, and then he insisted on playing . . . I wish I were sure he should be playing, now . . . It's — it's the most sporting thing I've ever known. I had to play well, at East Lake. I couldn't let Bobby down, you know.'
>
> Yes — I knew. And I know, too, that I saw something that afternoon at East Lake that will stand out as the prettiest picture of a lifetime in sport — the two greatest golfers, playing all they knew in every shot, in generous

*and gallant complement to one another, in the
greatest match I ever witnessed.*

Fourteen and sixteen are both straight and broad
and descend gently toward the lake, due west into
summer sunsets. They are like non-identical twins or
brother and sister — you can see the family resem-
blance but each has its own face and personality.
Today, the beautiful skyline of the city of Atlanta can
be seen from the sixteenth tee, six miles away; the
towers of the modern city shine in the morning sun.
But back in 1922, there was no visible evidence of a
city, since the Candler, Hurt, and Healey buildings —
at seventeen stories — were the tallest "skyscrapers"
in town.

Many members like the view from the sixteenth
tee more than any other, and if the golf score is now
hopeless and the match is over, it's a good place to
stop, take a picture of your guests, and ask your
friends to identify the buildings in the distance.

In 1922, when fourteen was the short par five on
the back nine, sixteen was a downhill 405-yard par
four. On September 16, 1922, during his record-setting round, Bobby drove 260 yards, hit a mashie-niblick twenty feet beyond the pin, sank the putt for
birdie three, and moved to eight under par.

SEVENTEEN

Seventeen is a 453-yard par four along the lake which asks for a drive over water to the right center of the fairway. Large fairway bunkers encourage the long hitter to drive to the left, which brings a tree on the left edge of the fairway and the greenside trap on that side into play. The entire hole is easy to see from the clubhouse on the left, and the rising ground on the right is perfect for spectators. The two finishing holes at East Lake will be exciting places when a close match is coming down to the wire.

Visually, the seventeenth is a treat all the way. It's a walk along the edge of the lake, and a good place to see East Lake's great blue heron, who likes to visit this spot.

Tommy loves telling about an old friend who thought he was fooling people when he moved his ball closer to the hole by placing his coin on the side toward the pin. He would spot the ball, clean it, place it, spot it, look at it, and place it again, edging closer and closer. One day on the seventeenth green of the Ryder Cup course (to the right of today's green), Tommy had spotted his ball on the green and was waiting for his partner, Jack Glenn, Jr., to play a bunker shot. The ball stopped four feet away and Tommy spotted the ball, while Jack raked the trap. He grinned at the others and called to his partner, "Jack, that's a great shot. If I could spot that ball two more times, you'd have a 'gimme' and we'd win this hole."

When you play with Tommy, after he's remembered a story and told it, you may get to enjoy hearing him repeat it several times for his own pleasure. He'll mutter part of it to himself as he stalks the rough looking for your ball, and he loves it when the real-life situation allows him to tell it again, slightly reworked to fit the current plot.

At age twenty, on September 16, 1922, Bobby played seventeen at 400 yards and drove 250 yards. His mashie approach was twenty feet away and he sank the putt for birdie three. That twenty foot birdie putt took him to nine under, lower than he had ever been before.

EIGHTEEN

About the eighteenth, a 232-yard par three, Colonel Jones said: "I know a one-shot finishing hole is not usually well regarded. But when a player stands on that tee at East Lake, with the match square or dormie — that drive calls for all there is, in the delicatessen department." Few balls will run up onto eighteen. The little "ridge by Ross," which guards so many greens at East Lake, demands that every inch be in the air.[14]

---

[14] Herbert Warren Wind once wrote about how Bobby described a bold shot under pressure which came off. RTJ, Jr. said it was "sheer delicatessen." Wonder where he got it.

Once Tommy was playing with Charlie Yates when Charlie hit an awful shot into the lake to cap off a bad day. Tommy was flabbergasted when Charlie ran down off the tee, made a beautiful racing dive from the ladies' tee and executed a perfect crawl at top speed to the other side.

Member Scott Hansen once came to eighteen with three guests. After taking a quick look from the blue tees, the one with the honor said, "Thank God, finally a short par four." Scott just chuckled and said, "Nope, it's a long par three." Later, on January 13, 1985, Scott was playing with Tommy Barnes against Don Russell and Bill Blalock. Scott took out his driver and hit a draw into the wind. The ball bounced on the green and ran into the hole for an ace. Scott and Tommy won the match one up.

In 1935, the match with Joyce Wethered wound up all square, thanks to Bobby's uphill fifteen foot par putt on the eighteenth green. He had a medal score of 71 that day despite his recent illness. Miss Wethered had 74, Charlie Yates 76, and young Dorothy Kirby 84, all playing from the back tees.

Late in the evening, on Saturday, September 16, 1922, twenty-year-old Bobby Jones and his father walked onto the eighteenth tee. He was nine under par. What was he thinking? Did he feel any pressure? Here are O.B. Keeler's words:

BOB JONES LOWERS HIS OWN RECORD AT EAST LAKE TO 63

Probably Greatest Round of Golf Ever Shot; Nine Birdies Included on Card

by O.B. Keeler

Two years ago, Bob Jones cut the course record at East Lake from 68 — set by himself — to 66, and has been shooting at it ever since. Four times he has equaled it, but he never could bust it.

And then, along in the cool of the evening of a waning September Saturday — yesterday, to be explicit — the patron saint of golf, St. Andrew, past question, took a good look at Bobby, as he started out with his dad and Tess Bradshaw and Abe Adair, and he said, said the good saint:

"Bobby, this is your day!"

And as night drew round about the match, dropping from the sky like a "feather from an eagle in his flight," Bobby stood on the last tee with a par 3 to make for a 63 — and he made it.

A 63, nine under fours. Nine over threes, if you prefer to put it that way. A miracle round. It was Bobby's day.

"I never played an easier round," Bobby confessed afterward. "That usually is the way, though. Your best scores come easily. You can't force them. When you work hard you don't score well. The ball rolls for you — or it doesn't. Dad and Brad and Abe were pretty much worked up, along on the last three holes, but I didn't feel worried at all until I stood on the last tee, and it was getting dark, and I thought for just a moment of all the things that might happen to that shot."

Iron Club - Iron Nerve

Just a moment. Then Bobby drew the trusty old driving iron, no wood for him on that shot. And through the thickening dusk the little white sphere bored its way, upheld by the backspin, climbing, climbing — to drop lightly, just at the right of the green, where Bobby's perfect chip shot, directed by his iron nerves, curled up dead at the cup, dead for a 3, and a 63 for the round, probably the greatest round of golf ever shot on as long and hard a course in the history of golf.

It was Bobby's day. St. Andrew was right. And so was Bobby. And I think the good old Saint smiled to himself as he rarely has smiled before, as the youngster with the tousled hair above his steady young face tapped the ball into the last cup and smiled at last upon his work, seeing that it was good.

Here is the card with par:

Par (Out) —	434	553	435	- 36		
Jones	324	443	434	- 31		
Par (In) —	434	455	443	- 36	– 72	
Jones	433	454	333	- 32	– 63	

Nine birdies. Nine holes in par. That's all. Not an eagle. Not a buzzard. The mistakes — save the mark — cost him birdies; a few. A missed putt of four feet on No. 3 — after perfect drive and pitch. A bunkered mashie on No. 7, the only trap he was in. A short approach and then a bit too strong a little pitch on No. 14, costing his only 5 of the round. That was the toll.

The Details

Perhaps the best way to commend that wonder round is just to give the detail, and here it is. You may clip this out and paste it in your scrapbook, for it is unlikely that you will ever see its like again, either in print or in the turf.

No. 1. 400 Yards, Par 4 — Drive. Spade mashie to 20 feet from the cup. One putt.

No. 2. 150 Yards, Par 3 — Spade mashie to one yard from the pin. One putt.

No. 3. 320 Yards, Par 4 — Drive of 290 yards. Wee pitch with mashie-niblick, to four feet from the pin. Missed putt. Took a four.

No. 4. 450 Yards, Par 5 — Long drive that ran into the rough at the elbow of the fairway. Iron to 25 feet from the pin. Two putts.

No. 5. 590 Yards, Par 5. — Drive 310 yards. Brassie 260 yards to edge of green. Chip dead. One putt.

No. 6. 175 Yards, Par 3 — Mashie to ten feet from the pin. Missed putt. Took par 3.

No. 7. 380 Yards, Par 4 — Drive.

Mashie to trap at left and in front of green. Niblick out to a yard from the pin. One putt.

No. 8. 230 Yards, Par 3 — Iron off to right in rough. Niblick to eight feet from cup. One putt.

No. 9. 525 Yards, Par 5 — Fair drive to heavy lie. Brassie short of green. Niblick chip to eight feet from cup. One putt.

Out in 31, a stroke better than his wonderful outward journey in one round of the recent southern championship. Bob took twelve putts on the nine greens, getting down with a single putt on six.

The Second Nine

No. 10. 425 Yards, Par 4 — Drive far up the hill. Mashie to ten feet of the cup. Missed putt, ball hitting cup. Took a 4.

No. 11. 175 Yards, Par 3 — Jigger to twenty feet from pin. Two putts.

No. 12. 390 Yards, Par 4 — Drive. Mashie-niblick to eight feet from cup. One putt.

No. 13. 380 Yards,

Par 4 — Drive 260 yards. Spade mashie to 20 feet from the cup. Two putts.

No. 14. 465 Yards, Par 5 — Drive 300 yards down alley. Mashie short of green, pin in front of green, and a wee pitch failed to stop promptly and rolled 15 feet past pin. Two putts.

No. 15. 505 Yards, Par 5 — Drive 260 yards. Brassie to edge of green, 30 feet from pin. Two putts.

No. 16. 405 Yards, Par 4 — Drive 260 yards. Mashie-niblick 20 feet past pin. One putt.

No. 17. 400 Yards, Par 4 — Drive 250 yards. Mashie 20 feet from pin. One putt.

No. 18. 205 Yards, Par 3 — Driving iron just off green at right. Chip dead. One putt.

Length of course from back tees as played; 6570 yards. Par 36 36 - 72. All putts holed. 12 putts going out; 14 coming in.

Paste It
In Your Book

File this with your records. Paste it on your club bulletin boards. You are not likely to see its like again. The bright Genius of Golf was on the blond brow of Bobby Jones the afternoon of Saturday, September 16, 1922, and the record he set at old East Lake, toughest championship course of the southland, is likely to endure until our generation has passed away.

"I don't believe I'll ever break it," said Bob simply.

It will be engraved in silver, too.

Eight years ago this month a silver cup was designed to bear the amateur records made at East Lake, the maker of each successive record to hold the cup until the record was broken by another. The first name on it is that of the late George Adair, a great name in southern golf. On September 8, 1914, Mr. Adair shot a 79, a new amateur record for the course just after it was remodeled in its present form.

The next name is that of D.E. Root, 78, July 2, 1915. Then Bob Jones took charge of the cup — and I suspect he will hold it from now on. The subsequent engravings read as follows:

R.T. Jones, Jr., 77, July 7, 1915

R.T. Jones, Jr., 74, July 4, 1916

R.T. Jones, Jr., 70, July 18, 1918

R.T. Jones, Jr., 69, July 16, 1919

R.T. Jones, Jr., 68, September 11, 1919

R.T. Jones, Jr., 66, September 13, 1920

Looking back now, the course record 63 at East Lake in 1922 seems like a turning point in the career of Bobby Jones. One week earlier, he had been beaten by Jess Sweetser 8-7 in a semifinal match in the U.S. Amateur at Brookline, which was the most decisive beating he'd ever taken in a national tournament. At age twenty, that defeat had been his eleventh national championship without a victory. However, in the years stretching before him, he would set an incredible pace and turn the world of golf completely upside down, forever. He was destined to win thirteen national championships in only eight years, an unbelievable sixty-two percent of the ones he entered. He would finish, in 1930, with the Grand Slam of Golf, all four British and American national titles in one year. In almost exactly eight years from that day at East Lake, on Saturday, September 27, 1930, he would win his last match at Merion for his fifth U.S. Amateur championship and complete the Grand Slam. He would retire from competition at age twenty-eight as an international hero and be the only person to have two ticker-tape parades on Broadway. But in September of 1922, he was suffering through the end of what O.B. Keeler later called his "seven lean years." In a week, he would give up golf for the season and enter Harvard to work toward a second bachelor's degree. His next golf tournament would be the U.S. Open of 1923, which was destined to become his first national championship victory.

II

More About the Colonel
Robert P. Jones
1879 - 1956

*M*arion Williams grew up in Cochran, Georgia, and later moved to Atlanta and married Ralph Williams, who was a longtime law partner of Bobby's. She and her husband were close friends of the family. When she was a child she remembers that the man she knew all of her life as Big Bob came to hunt birds with her father, James Peter Peacock. "Big Bob was the only man I ever heard call my father *Pete*."

They were known as Big Bob and Little Bob because that's what Miss Clara [Bobby's mother] always called them. She called Bob Little Bob all of his life. I never saw a father and son so close and so sympathetic to one another. All of their lives they would kiss each other on greeting and Bob visited his father every single day, even late in his life when he had to use his rolling chair. Big Bob had an elevator installed so his son could get to him whenever he wanted.

Big Bob loved to sing. I remember that he stood under the big old oak tree in front of the clubhouse in Augusta and sang 'Ole Man River' across that beautiful land, accompanied on the harmonica by Mrs. Doud, Mamie Eisenhower's mother. They had a wonderful time together, and so did everybody who was watching and listening.

He hated to drive and employed a chauffeur, but he never sat in the back like he was a big-shot. I remember seeing them riding down Peachtree. They always looked like they were shouting at each other, constantly arguing — I think mostly about baseball.

His favorite story on himself concerned his well known profanity and his secretary, Miss Kate, who was the most proper and demure old maid. Once he yelled from his desk, 'Miss Katie, you've just got to find that goddamned trust indenture.' After looking all over the place, she came back and announced, 'Mr.

Jones, I can't find that goddamned trust indenture.' Big Bob would laugh his head off every time he told that story.

III

MORE ABOUT BOBBY

*O*ne of the fondest memories that Charlie Yates and Tommy Barnes share relates to an event in 1937. Bobby was in a gallery with his two Atlanta friends watching Ray Billows in the final round of the U.S. Amateur in Portland, Oregon. After Billows hit a perfect recovery shot around a tree to the green with a five iron, Bobby said to his friends, loud enough for the player and several spectators to hear: "That's a great shot. I don't think anyone in the world but Ray Billows could play that shot."

An old man nearby objected: "Mister, you don't know what you're talking about. Bobby Jones could do that with his eyes closed."

Bobby smiled: "I'm certain that he could not."

The man persisted, "Mister, did you ever see that sonofabitch play?"

Bobby just shook his head and laughed with everyone else. He never let on and told the man who he was; he just walked away, smiling. He must have loved not being recognized. That way he could be *with* people and enjoy them, not above them and distant.

Although the golfing career of Bobby Jones attracted the attention of the world, the most remarkable feature of his life was its diversity and balance. He had an unusual education, which reflected the culture and expectations of his family, as well as his own intellectual drive. In 1922, Bobby graduated from Georgia Tech with a degree in Mechanical Engineering. Then, during the same years that he won many of his national championships, he received a second bachelor's degree at Harvard in English Literature (1924), attended Emory Law School (1926-1927), and passed the Bar exam. The result was his long career as an attorney after he retired from competition at age twenty-eight. Those who were privileged to practice with him know some wonderful details that illuminate his personality.

Harvey Hill was a law partner of Bobby's. He remembers the first time he saw him — about 1920 in the Southern Amateur at East Lake.

I picked him up on the fourth tee. He hit a ball off that tee which was the longest shot I'd ever seen. But nobody could find the ball. They looked all over and finally found it over by the fence on the right. Bob walked over, took a good look, and pulled out his baffey. Then he took a big swing, and the ball sailed clear up onto the green over 200 yards away. The crowd went wild.

I played lots of golf with Bob, but in the twenties and thirties we couldn't get him away from East Lake; he was always over there. Later, during the forties, East Lake began to get crowded and he would play with us sometimes on Sunday morning at Capital City. One day I played with Richard Garlington against Bob and Charlie Black. We played the back nine first that day, and they closed us out with three holes to go. After I paid my five dollars I went up to Bob on the seventh tee and said, 'Well, Bob, you've beaten us bad. Now I want to play you for five dollars a hole from here on in.'

Bob turned to me: 'You mean that, Harvey?'

'I sure do,' I said, 'and you've got to give me a shot on every one since they're all 'stroke' holes for me.' I was pretending to be upset.

'All right, then, I'll do it if that's what you want.' He looked real serious.

The seventh was a par five, the eighth a par

four, and the ninth a par five. I played some of my best golf and shot three straight pars, but it wasn't good enough. On the par five seventh, he drove to the top of the hill, hit a fairway wood onto the green, and sank the putt for eagle three. One up. On the eighth, a 350-yard par four, Bob drove the green by hitting up onto the hill to the left and having it trickle down to the green. He made that putt for eagle two. Two up. On the par five ninth, he drove almost to the top of the hill, reached the green with his second, and made the final putt for his third straight eagle. After he pulled his ball out of the cup, he turned to me, 'I guess that'll teach you a lesson.' He was not smiling.

Bobby's temper was famous, but Harvey Hill and all who knew him emphasize one important feature. He could be hard on himself, his peers, and the rich and famous, but he was always courteous to less prominent people and charming to strangers and vulnerable younger associates. The big-shots and everyone else loved him — no one can remember any attack on the weak; he never tried to build himself up by demeaning those who were less fortunate.

He never used people. Harvey remembers that Bobby's law practice was a lot smaller than it could have been if he had taken advantage of his influence around the world to bring in new business.

*Many times I would come to him and say,
'Bob, why don't you call so-and-so and see if
we can be of any help, you know him so well.'
He said: 'I'll get around to it in a little while,'
but he never did. He never used his influence to
manipulate people. That's why we all admired
him so much; he was so lacking in affectation
and always so genuine.*

Eugene Branch is an Atlanta attorney and a member of the Atlanta Athletic Club. He was also in Bobby's law firm.

*I was mostly a tennis player and I remember
Bob telling me that I ought to play golf
because it was more relaxing — 'You just can't
think of anything else while you're playing
golf.'*

*Bob was a great friend of Robert Woodruff's.[15]
Mr. Woodruff was a good golfer and I remember his favorite Bobby Jones story. One day he
was playing the Old Course at St. Andrews
with a caddie who said very little. On one hole
he hit three great shots to a par five and was
about three feet away. He turned to the caddie*

---

[15] Robert W. Woodruff was Chairman of the Coca-Cola Company. He became Atlanta's greatest benefactor after he retired.

and said, 'That was a pretty good shot, wasn't it?' The caddie uttered his first words, 'When Bobby Jones played this hole he was there in two.' He thought he would pull the leg of the caddie a little and said, 'Who's Bobby Jones?' At that, the caddie just laid down his bag and walked off the golf course; he never said another word.

Gene remembers a comment that Bobby made about his name: "I asked Bob how he felt about people calling him Bobby, since he seemed to prefer the more mature Bob."

"It's not any big deal, but let me show you something." He pulled out a letter he'd saved which was from a grammar school teacher. Apparently the teacher had asked the students to write a letter to a famous person, and the letter went as follows:

Dear Bobby,

I'm in the third grade and when I grow up I want to be an engineer. What are you going to be when you grow up?

Bob turned to me, 'This kid thinks I'm his age.'

Gene said that Bobby told him he was always asked about who the greatest player was, and he remembered that some Scots used to say, "Old Tom Morris could beat Bobby Jones if he had the same equipment and played the same golf courses." Bob said: "I always thought this was a useless argument. The only thing you can do is beat the people playing against you; there's no way you can work on somebody who died before you were born or who was born after you died."

I remember one time that I had the great idea of naming one of our new courses at the Athletic Club Calamity Jane. I couldn't wait to go to work the next morning so I could tell Bob about it. But I could tell he didn't like the idea at all. When I thought about it I realized he didn't like anything that tended to glorify something about him. He was the most humble person.

I always thought the most impressive piece of information about Bob was that when he was thirteen he won the championships of both the East Lake Country Club and the Druid Hills Golf Club. At first I thought the person telling me must have meant the junior championships, but I was wrong. He won the 'real' club championships at age thirteen. There is a gold watch at our club which was presented to him in 1915 by the membership in commemoration of those two victories.

Ralph Williams came to work at Jones, Bird, and Howell in 1958 when Bobby Jones was fifty-six.

There was a big difference in our ages, but I did work for him and certainly enjoyed getting to know him. One of the things I remember most clearly was how Bob always knew the name of any new secretary or young associate who joined the firm. He'd be wheeled by in his wheelchair and when the newcomers passed him in the hall Bob would always call them by name and look them right in the eye. All those young people considered that a great compliment.

Bob Jones and his daddy were real close. They especially loved leaving work early in the afternoon to play golf together at East Lake. Occasionally they would ask a third or a fourth to join them, but mainly they liked to be by themselves. They loved doing anything together.

I know the reason that Bob Jones gave up practicing law. Once he was trying a case, and during the recess of a day or two, the judge asked him to play golf. This was during the thirties and he was certainly a world-famous figure at that point. Later, when he got a favorable verdict he wondered whether the decision had come his way because of his name and reputation. When he got back to the office, he told my father [Ralph Williams, Sr.] that he wouldn't go into court anymore. He had decided that his reputation could give him an advantage and that his opponents might not receive fair treatment.

He didn't practice even on business matters after the fifties, and basically managed his own investments. These included a string of Coca-Cola bottling plants up in New England. At that time, he had decided he wanted to sell the plants and he sent me up there to negotiate the sales. I made many trips and spent all week up there talking to this person or that person, trying to work out the proper deal. When I came back I always went over to his house and left off all the details on the Friday or Saturday. I used to dread Monday morning because I knew that he would want the details word-for-word. It was a lot harder answering his questions than making those deals in New England. When it finally came time to close the deal, I spent many more hours negotiating the precise words of the contract with Bob than with the other side. He was an absolute perfectionist and a master of the English language. Also, he had an incredible memory and a wonderful capacity for complex details. He never forgot a thing.

Ralph remembers one of Bobby's favorite letters, in which a friend had written to him, "I apologize for writing such a long letter, but I didn't have time to make it shorter."

After his playing days, Bobby was frequently invited to appear with other figures from what has been called "the golden age of sport," the 1920's. One event was recorded by Fred Russell, the longtime Sports Editor of *The Nashville Banner*, in his book *Bury Me In an Old Press Box*. The occasion was a luncheon in September of 1953 in Nashville with Jack Dempsey and Red Grange, which was described by Bill Corum of *The New York Journal American*.

Red Grange, a still slim and racy-looking man with dark auburn hair, thinning a little now, moved into the big room. Once he was as close to a darting, spinning shaft of light across the cross bars of a football field as any man has ever been before or since — now it was the big fellow, Jack Dempsey. There's something about that Dempsey, forever boyish. Through the archway came a man walking slowly with a cane. A proud man, in the way that a man should be proud in face of whatever may befall him. Suddenly, every man in the room was on his feet. Hand clapping drew as close to a cheer as the clapping of hands can come. Tears jumped to sting a little behind your eyes. Bobby Jones smiled. 'Thank you gentlemen,' he said. And then, turning the moment deftly, as the champions and those who are born with such a knack can do, he said: 'But I know why you are applauding. I'm the only man in the room who had the foresight to bring his high-ball with him from the bar. It was a fine thing, a very fine thing. Not many men, whatever they may have done, ever got a tribute so truly spontaneous and touching.'

Fred Russell continued:

Even in Bob's sense of humor, always there was a certain softness. He had been intrigued by the veteran caddies at St. Andrews when he won the British Amateur in 1930. 'In experience, wisdom, and dignity, they're in a group to themselves,' he once told me. There was one, perhaps seventy, carrying the clubs of an unpleasant fellow who was playing very poor golf and blaming it all on the caddie. The old caddie maintained a dignified silence, of course — until the man formally declared, addressing the other members of the match: 'For this round, I believe I've drawn the worst caddie in the world!' 'Oh no, Sir,' said the caddie. 'That would be quite too great a coincidence.'

IV

MY LOVE AFFAIR
WITH EAST LAKE
by Charlie Elliott

I played my first game of golf on the East Lake course in 1935, and I played my last game there in 1994, shortly after it had been purchased by Tom Cousins. During those years, I became wedded to East Lake. I followed a golf ball over many layouts across this country, but never found another one with the charm, dignity, and challenge of the old No. 1 course at East Lake.

My golf was always a long drive from championship caliber, but I do remember a few special shots, such as the double eagle on number five, when par there was five, and on number six, the island hole, where my tee shot bounced off the flagstick and stopped half an inch away, the nearest I ever came to a hole-in-one.

The best score I ever shot at East Lake was when I played one time in a foursome with Bob Jones and Charlie Yates and another golfer. I remember that a couple of pros were supposed to play, and they called at the last moment to cancel. I had no game, was not planning to play, and was on the club veranda having a beer, when Bob asked me to join the match and make it a foursome.

"You know I don't play that kind of golf," I told him.

"You are not lousy enough to hold up the game too much," he said. "I'll take you as a partner and we'll try them."

I am sure that one reason I remember the game was that it was the best score I ever shot at East Lake. I can only guess I didn't want to show how much of a dub I really was, and concentrated on looking at and hitting the ball. Also, they gave me quite a few putts I probably would have missed. I remember that I shot a 68, and didn't figure in a hole. The other scores were as low or lower than mine, but Bob shot one of his best rounds, and sank his last putt for a 64.

I played with [Robert W.] Woodruff and Jones at both East Lake and over the Peachtree course, but cannot remember the details of any of those matches, except that Woodruff always took Jones as a partner. No one objected, because we never played for more than a golf ball or a dollar, and Woodruff always picked up the tab for caddie fees and drinks.

Most of all, I remember the fellowship of the delightful companions who strode down the fairways with me through the years, when golf was a walking game with caddies and not dependent on vehicular transportation from shot to shot.

No matter how beautiful a golf course is, or how well you strike the ball, unless you are a pro with an eye for a purse, the main pleasure and worth to be gotten from playing is the competitive fellowship of friends and associates who are special people in your life.

For years I played regularly with Bob Jones over the East Lake course. Because of his qualities of shot making under pressure, the smooth, sweet poetry of his swing, his complete integrity, and his charm as an individual, many consider him the greatest golfer since the game began. Once he insisted on calling a shot on himself when he was the only person who saw his ball move as he addressed it. That added a stroke, which cost him a major tournament.

If you didn't know of his celebrity, you'd never suspect it when you played with him. The quality of his shotmaking was still with him, but he was so down-to-earth, so considerate of those with him, so human in every way, that you would consider him only as a delightful member of your foursome, all the way through the nineteenth hole.

In the nineteenth hole, I never failed to do my share when we sat around the locker-room table and held delightful post-mortems. Our little bailiwick was always the most fragrant corner of the locker-room. Bob's favorite drink was good corn whisky, and one of my old-time mountain neighbors helped me keep him supplied with the pure corn, made only from meal and cornsprouts, with no other catalytic ingredients such as sugar or yeast.

I put a two-gallon oak keg in Bob's locker and kept it filled with corn. It had an insignificant leak that perfumed the area. Even Pierce Harris, the minister who had a locker among us infidels but was a complete teetotaler, admitted that he enjoyed the fragrance in that corner of the room.

Bob played golf all over the world, in both competitive and friendly matches, but his favorite golfing layout at any and all times was the No. 1 course at East Lake. He started playing there when he was six years old, and his last few games, before he was stricken with a nerve disorder and forced to retire in his middle forties, were at East Lake.

Another golfer who was one of my longtime favorites as a partner, opponent, and friend, was Watts Gunn. Wattsy and I played in countless matches together. He was a brilliant shot-maker. I remember that about a third of the time when he made a good shot, the hat would fly off the back of his head, and a bad shot would cause him to swear his favorite cuss word, "Jeepers!," which was the most vulgar term I ever heard him use.

Watts and I played with many men who were

famous or noted in their endeavors, though not necessarily in golf. One that I vividly recall was W.D. "Bo" Randall. Bo was the owner of several orange groves in Florida, but his chief claim to fame was his Randall-made knives. His cutlery was so much in demand that his factory in Orlando was never able to keep up with the orders. The knife he made for the U.S. Marine Corps was said to be the finest military knife ever manufactured.

Bo had a fascinating weakness for lost golf balls — not those lost by him, but by other people. We played many rounds of golf at East Lake, but I'm sure he never set foot on one of the fairways there, except to cross it from rough to green. He kept his shots down the middle, and his caddie was able to walk straight to them. Bo walked from the tee to his ball on the edge of the rough, and after his second shot, which usually landed on or near the green, he made his way to the ball through the rough. His main pleasure in playing seemed to be finding lost golf balls. He was wealthy enough to buy any golf ball factory and give it away, but his day was highly successful only if he came back to the clubhouse with a pocketful of old balls. We often wondered what he did with them. I never saw him hit any ball but one that was new or had been played only a few holes.

A regular member of our Saturday morning foursome for many years was Charlie Yates. Charlie had won many tournaments and was one of the most noted of the amateur champions, with the British Amateur as one of his wins. For years we had a friendly game every Saturday morning at East Lake with Dr. Pierce Harris, a renowned Methodist minister, and Bill Murray, a very good golfer and prominent businessman. I was the heathen in that foursome. Every Sunday morning, while Yates and Murray were regular attendants at the church where Dr. Harris presided, I played golf in another foursome with Tommy Barnes, Billy Street, and Ernest Harrison. Dr. Harris was aware of this transgression and told me several times, "You are the worst member of my church, and if you knew some of the members you'd resent that."

I well remember Colonel Bob Jones, who was Bob's father. The Colonel made up for his lack of skill with his colorful language. There was nothing vicious about it, or ugly, but he knew all the words and seemed to find a lot of satisfaction in using them.

Tommy Barnes was the best golfer in our Sunday morning foursome, but the rare character in this group was our Mr. Harrison. Ernest was an excellent golfer, with just enough information about the rules to start an argument after every wayward shot, especially those with untenable lies. Once he was just off the fairway, where a dog had scratched to cover its leavings.

"I can drop out of here," Ernest announced.

"Why?" he was asked.

"The rule book says I can move out of a hole made by a burrowing animal."

"That was made by a dog," Street said.

"Everyone knows that a dog is a burrowing animal," Harrison replied.

He continued to argue about it even after we had refused to allow him relief and he had lost the hole. This was written up in a national magazine and credited to someone else, but I was there and heard the original version.

Among the many topics we discussed during our games was the news that men had landed on the moon.

"That's a lot of foolishness and a complete waste of our money," Ernest declared. "Pretty soon they'll have some guy landing on the sun."

"You dumb bastard," Barnes said. "Do you know how hot the sun is?"

"Sure I do," our partner replied. "But they can always land up there at night."

One of the unforgettable characters in the early days at East Lake was Stewart Maiden. I knew the old pro only for a brief time during his last years, when he was pro at Peachtree Golf Club in north Atlanta, but heard much about him from Bob Jones. When he was seven or eight years old and just starting golf, Bob copied the "Maiden swing" and went through his entire golfing career with the smoothest, easiest stroke, that was almost poetry in its rhythm.

Bob told me many stories about the old pro's sense of humor. Once, when a member was taking lessons,

Stewart suddenly stopped him, caught his student's wrist in an iron grip and asked, "Do you *have* to play golf?"

Another time, the pro, commenting to one of his clients during a play-practice round, said, "You're a damn fine golfer, you've just got one failing. You can't get the ball in the hole."

There's a well known and much repeated story that when Jones was in a major championship at Oakmont, he started trying to guide his shots and was missing them just enough to land in all sorts of trouble. Maiden listened to the radio reports and sent Bob a wire: "Hit hell out of them. They'll go somewhere." Bob said he followed this advice, and while many of his shots were still off line, he was hitting them over and beyond the trouble spots.

I played golf with Jones during the last few of his club-throwing days, and saw him only a few times when he was so completely exasperated with a stroke that he tossed a club into the air. He was such a fierce competitor that it was frustration with himself, and we all understood it. He completely conquered this tendency in his final years.

Another member of the East Lake staff who came along in my time, and for whom I had a great deal of affection and respect, was Jimmy Brett. Jimmy was caddie master and official starter for twenty-eight years at East Lake, and later moved on to the Atlanta Athletic Club's new course at Riverview. Regardless of the weather, overflow of players, and other adverse conditions, he never failed to keep play going smoothly over the course. For many reasons he was a member favorite. He treated everyone with the same pair of gloves. Jones told me that once, when he was President of the Athletic Club and in a hurry to get through a round and meet a business appointment, he asked Brett to move his starting time ahead of another foursome. "I'm sorry, Mr. Jones," Jimmy said, "but they came in and registered ahead of you, and you'll have to wait your turn."

Another one of my favorite employees over many years was Dave Williams, who kept the locker room and the clubhouse going for almost fifty years. He knew every member, and most of their families. His income included tips as well as his salary. I knew Dave for years before I discovered that his income was more impressive than I had realized. Often when I had discarded a pair of shoes or an old suit I took them out to Dave. Then, once, when I came in with some shirts and worn trousers that I thought might help him, I noticed his worried expression.

"You look upset," I said. "Is anything wrong?"

"Yes sir," he said. "I guess I am worried. The furnace in one of my apartment houses has gone on the blink and I can't find anybody to fix it."

I learned later that he had collected, saved, and invested enough money over the years to be as wealthy as many of the members he served in the locker room.

I remember that Bob was an opera fan and attended and contributed to the operas in Atlanta, but Bob and I never discussed music. He never indicated to me whether his contributions were for his love of music itself, or because of his support for this fine art. He gave me a charming little book, *Opera Guyed*, by Newman Levy, published by Alfred Knopf in 1933. It was a burlesque and poetry on the opera stories. He indicated that two of his favorites in this book were "Thaïs" and "Carmen."

If Bob loved anything more than his family or golf, it was fishing. He got so excited when he landed a fish that a time or two I thought I'd have to give him artificial respiration or some form of first aid.

I have no record of the dates when Bob and I started fishing together, but I know he was still able to navigate on a golf course. We golfed and fished together for ten years or more, until he became unable to handle a golf club, and then we switched over to fishing completely. I'm sure we did some lakeside fishing for bream, but most of our fishing was from a boat. We wet our lures in many places in north Florida, on the Georgia coast, in the mountains, and in the large lakes closer to home. When he got to the point when he could no longer maneuver well in the ordinary fishing skiff, I built an eighteen-foot fishing boat to include a swivel bow seat with shelf and storage space within easy reach of his hands. We used this until his fingers became so crippled that he was unable to handle a fishing reel or rod.

Bob was interested in everything outdoors, and even while we fished we watched and identified birds and other creatures, and a few times we stopped casting to follow a deer swimming across one arm of a lake.

A big chunk of pleasure went out of my life when Bob and I had to give up fishing together.

These are a few of the memories I cherish from my love affair of sixty years with the club and golf course at East Lake.

V

One Down with
One to Play [16]
by Henry A. McCusker

$\mathcal{T}$he sign on the fence read "Private Property — No Trespassing." But one side of the gate was open so I drove through and continued down the driveway toward the clubhouse. This was my first visit to the East Lake Country Club and I was surprised to see such an unbecoming sign. It put the place on the defensive, I thought, and then with my first glimpse of the clubhouse — a huge Tudor-like structure, dark and brooding in the distance — I was at once reminded of similar signs and structures I had seen twenty-two years before, in 1959, when I first came to Atlanta.

Those signs were along Washington Street in front of large decaying old houses which three quarters of a century earlier must have been the residences of the

---

[16] This story was the result of a visit to East Lake by the author in 1981. That was in the middle of the twenty-five year period between its time as the golf course of the Atlanta Athletic Club and the formation of East Lake Golf Club.

fashionable establishment. The houses still possessed faint traces of their once-grand character, seemingly unwilling to yield entirely to increasing hard use and neglect by generations of other occupants. But nothing remains of those old houses now, not even their ghosts.

Fortunately, the notion which got into my head far exceeded the extent to which East Lake had deteriorated. Its best days were long past to be sure, but clues to its built-in high quality were instantly visible, and, it seemed to me, that unlike those old houses, this crusted old diamond was now being nurtured rather than abused.

I decided to park the car and walk around in order to get a closer look at things, and I began to feel a little ashamed for having allowed twenty-two years to go by before coming out here to see Bobby Jones' home course. I have played golf since 1945 and I love the game; I have seen all the current great players many times and I never miss the Masters. How could I not have come out here long ago to see where Bobby Jones started playing golf — where he grew up, practiced, and perfected his game, that man who was born an invalid and died an invalid, but had been the greatest player of his time, a super person, and a genuine national hero?

There was not a good answer to that question but I consoled myself with the thought that now I would appreciate East Lake even more. For not only had I read more about Bobby Jones during those years, but I myself had become a better player and gained some small awareness of the pressures in tournament golf. For those reasons, my feeling of appreciation and esteem for the spirit of his old place would be keener and of greater value.

After leaving the car in the lot behind the clubhouse, I walked around to the front without seeing anyone. It was late October and the weather was cloudy, windy, and damp — not a good day for golf. The first tee was to the left of where I stood directly in front of the clubhouse, but there were no golfers around. Then a lone middle-aged man emerged from some shrubbery behind me. He had been picking up bits of paper trash and showed a little embarrassment over having been observed tidying up, or the place needing it. He smiled, said good morning, and we introduced ourselves and shook hands. He said, "What brings you out here?" I answered, "The memory of Bobby Jones."

It crossed my mind that he might take what I said to mean that I had known the great golfer personally, so I was quick to correct a possible misunderstanding. But he had not misunderstood at all and seemed to know that what brought me here was a feeling of profound respect and awe for a man he felt the same way about. The difference was that he had known Bobby Jones and played several rounds of golf with him right here at East Lake. That was after the war when Jones was in his forties and near the end of his playing days.

I felt comfortable with this man I had just met and as we talked we walked around some. I gauged him to be typical of the men who are still members of East Lake: loyal and proud of the club's distinguished past, honored and inspired by the courage and deeds of its great hero, aware of the club's decline but determined to continue the struggle against almost overwhelming economic and social forces threatening to end the club's existence. And I could understand it all, especially after seeing as much as I did of the course. I felt that the course was getting hold of me somehow, through its sheer showing of itself. Just as a star creates its own light and warmth, this place created its own aura of time and patience and beauty. East Lake was old, artful, and surprising. The cult of haste and greed could never see it as I did, but, taken on its own terms, I believed that Nature had accepted this course and that it deserved to be restored and preserved, not destroyed in the name of progress.

We returned to the first tee area and still there were no golfers around. The member told me that two of his friends would be here soon and asked if I would like to make it a foursome and play as his guest. I said that I would like nothing better, but I could not, and I explained that I was expected home soon, and besides I did not have my clubs with me. But I made a strong bid for a raincheck and he readily obliged me. We exchanged business cards and he said that whenever I could play I should call him. I thanked him, said that I definitely would, and left.

A little more than three weeks went by before I called him at his place of business downtown — a brokerage house. He seemed glad to hear from me. (East Lake was looking for new members and he might try to sell some stock for me as well.) We wasted no time getting to the point of my call. "When would you like to play?" he asked.

"Today." I answered.

"Today?" he gasped. "There's no way I can play today."

I said, "That's all right. I understand. But how would it be if I played alone?" In order to give him time to think about that I went on talking and I explained that I was calling from the lunchroom at the Stone Mountain course, that I had taken the day off and came over here intending to play, but when I arrived I thought of East Lake and the more I thought of it the more I felt compelled to call. (Ordinarily, playing golf alone is no fun for me, but I knew the first round at East Lake would be more than just golf. It would be a trip into the past as well, and that did not have to be shared to be enjoyed. In fact, by playing alone I would be better able to feel the aesthetic depths of the place.) He asked for a number of the phone I was using and said he would call me right back. After a few minutes he did call and said, "It's all set. I just talked to the pro and there's not much going on out there today. You can start playing as soon as you get there — just check in with the pro and he will take care of you."

I thanked him and when I hung up the phone I exclaimed, "Hot Damn" so loudly I startled several people in the lunchroom.

Stone Mountain State Park and Downtown Atlanta are connected by fifteen miles of Memorial Drive, and East Lake is situated along this route two-thirds of the way in. I covered the ten miles in what must have been record time for that time of day, and while I felt exhilarated over the prospect of playing, I was also somewhat depressed by the neighbor-hoods along this toward-town direction. It was, after all, East Lake's nearness to the inner-city that brought on its present-day plight. And it was also in my mind that if I were to continue on Memorial Drive the remaining five miles I would pass Oakland Cemetery, the city's oldest burial ground, where Bobby Jones was laid to rest in 1971. His grave is just inside the cemetery's south wall which runs along Memorial Drive (a few blocks from City Hall and the State Capitol). It seemed that Bobby Jones and East Lake were inseparable in my mind now and my thoughts of them had become a little sad, almost mournful.

But that brief heavy feeling evaporated when I drove through East Lake's gate. The disagreeable sign on the fence went unnoticed this time, and upon seeing the clubhouse and grounds, I felt a little like Hugh Conway must have felt when he reached Shangri-La the second time. Nobody was on the first tee and I could not wait to start playing. The weather was something like it had been the first time I was here — very cloudy and damp, but not windy or cold. However, a cold front was due to move through later in the afternoon or evening, bringing with it clear skies and dry, much colder air.

Within a few minutes I had parked the car, changed shoes, checked in with the pro, strapped my golf bag to the electric cart he had waiting for me, and drove to the first tee. I did take time to loosen up (in lieu of hitting practice balls) and, in honor of the occasion, broke open a pack of three new Wilson Pro Staffs. I must have been feeling reverence for the place which resulted in excellent concentration because I hit a good solid drive down the center of the fairway about 240 yards. I had the feeling I was going to play very well.

The second shot presented no particular problem. The ball was sitting up and the distance to the pin looked to be about 180 yards. The score card showed the first hole to be 420 yards and what I had left looked like a four-iron shot. The pin was on the right side of the green behind a trap and I intended to hit the ball to the left of the pin into the center of the green. But the ball went straight at the flag and fell short of the green and into the trap. Before getting back into the cart I noticed that to the right of where I stood there was a flag, about fifty yards away beyond and below some trees. It had to be the second green. I could see tee markers to the right of the green I just played to, so the second must be a par three coming back this way. I drove the cart toward the second green thinking that I would just see how far back the pin was before having to play my next tee shot. But, as I looked in that direction my vision and attention were carried beyond the green another thirty yards or so to the third tee where a man stood, waiting. I was surprised to see him there, or anyone, and thought it strange that the pro made no mention of another single golfer being out here a hole or two ahead of me. Neither of us waved nor made any gesture to indicate the other's presence.

After looking over the layout around that green I continued on my way to finish the first hole. I parked the cart near the tee, took my sand wedge and putter, and walked over to play my third shot. My golfer friends know me to be very good at getting out of sand traps. In fact, one of them once said that I must be the guy who taught Gary Player how to use the sand wedge. Playing the sand shot is the single best part of my game and the shot I played here was in keeping with that. I blasted out three feet from the cup and even left myself an easy uphill putt which I promptly sank for a par four. Today would be especially good for playing out of traps because the surface of the sand was smooth and hard, left that way by a day of light rain. A good trap player can really put "stop" on the ball he hits from wet sand.

I was not thinking about that as I moved on to the tee. My back had been toward the second green and the third tee for a while and I wondered if the man was still waiting. I turned and looked in his direction and he was there all right and still watching me. I believed that he had seen where I hit my first drive, watched my second shot, my third from the sand and the short putt, and probably concluded that since I was not a hacker it would be worth his while to wait for me and not have to play alone. Or maybe he was a hustler waiting to catch a "fish" — me. (In 1974 I spent two weeks in Dallas on business and a hustler there picked on me. We played three times, and it was a good thing for him that there was not a fourth time because, by then, I probably would have become the new owner of half of his trucking company.) The distance to the pin on this short hole was not more than a five-iron shot, but I hit it fat and the ball fell short of the green. However, the chip shot was exceptionally good, the ball stopping six inches from the cup — so close that there was no need to putt out. I picked up the ball and walked to the third tee. The man had not taken his eyes off me and when I got close to him he smiled and said, "Would you like some company, sir?"

His voice, looks, and demeanor were those of a well-bred young man. This was no hustler, I thought, not the usual kind anyway. "Sure thing," I said. He had a carrying bag so I told him he could strap it next to mine and share the cart with me.

"That's swell, thank you sir," he said.

"My name is Harry McCusker," I told him and held out my hand.

"Mine is Bob Clara," he said with a very firm handshake. I was about to ask him to spell his last name because I had not heard *Clara* as a last name before and I thought the spelling might be something else. But he was already saying that I should take the honor and hit first because anyone who played the first two holes as well as I did deserved it. I knew he was being polite. Nothing had been said about our playing a match but my instincts told me that one was about to begin, and that he would be some kind of player. His first words to me, "Would you like some company, sir?" were a challenge, I felt, as well as a question — conveyed in the way a medieval knight would have gone about enticing a stranger into friendly combat. He looked very fit, in the prime of life, and about twenty-eight years old.

The third hole was a 370-yard par four which ran along the club's property line to the right. Hitting to the right had to be avoided because of trees and a fence, but there was also a long fairway sand trap covering what would have otherwise been a good place to hit the drive. The only place left was a narrow strip of fairway just left of that sand, but a ball hit too far in that direction would carry into some other trees. I judged that distance to be not more than I could hit with the driver, especially today with the course being as soft as it was, and I hit a good straight drive to the desired spot. Being unfamiliar with the course, it had taken a few moments for me to figure all that out before I hit, but Bob Clara required no time at all. He took his three-wood from the bag and slammed the ball on the same line mine had taken and it landed ten yards ahead of mine and just short of being in the trees. I hit a six-iron second shot twelve feet from the flag. He hit an eight-iron to the back of the green and two-putted for a four. I sank the twelve-footer for a birdie three.

He was sincere in the compliment he paid me and as we rode to the next tee it was in my mind that I should be the one to somehow make it official now that we were playing a match, since I had taken first blood so to speak. The stakes, if any, were unimportant, but pride and one-on-one competition were very important and, I suspected, more so to him than to me. So, as I stepped onto the tee, I turned to him and said, "I'm one up."

He looked at me and said, "There you go," which I long ago came to know is a Southern response meaning complete affirmation.

From that point on occurred some of the best golf I have ever seen or will ever see. While I played better than I am really capable of playing, Bob Clara was absolutely unbelievable. He hit a drive on the fourth (a long par five hole) the likes of which I had not seen before. The impact sounded like a thunderclap and the ball leaped off the club face as if it had been fired from a cannon, and it did not come down until it had carried at least 285 yards. His three-wood second shot was likewise struck with great force. The ball did not get higher than thirty feet above the ground and was hit so straight that the sight of it against the dark sky made me think of a tracer-bullet — which is something I had not seen nor thought of since 1944 when I was flying bombing missions over Germany. It came down on the soft green about fifteen feet from the pin. My third shot landed in the trap on the right side of the green, and although I managed to get down in two from the sand, my par five was two strokes more than his eagle three. "That was really something — the way you played that hole," I said to him. He looked very pleased but said only, "Thank you," and seemed to want to let it go at that.

But I continued, "Only a very unusual golfer can hit shots like those . . . ," and I was again about to inquire into the spelling of his last name as a means of getting to his identity as a golfer. But he had walked onto the fifth tee and was getting ready to hit. (It was not necessary for either of us to say anything about the match being even again.) I watched him very carefully as he hit his drive and realized that his golf game was to a Rolls Royce as mine was to a Chevrolet. There was really no comparison — he was definitely world-class and I could live to be a hundred and not ever hit the ball the way he did. What perfection he had in timing, balance, concentration, grace, and power. Still, golf is a game of how many, as they say, not how, and after the fifth hole the match was still even — halved in fours. (I had missed the green with my second shot but chipped to within eight feet of the cup and made the putt. He was on the green in two and just missed a twenty-footer for a birdie.) I knew that if I were to stay in this match I would have to be very lucky, stay cool, and take advantage of whatever small opening might come my way. After all, the best golfer in any tournament or match does not always win and, as Bobby Jones himself used to say, anything can happen.

I went one up again on the 175-yard par three sixth hole thanks to a spectacular five-iron shot I hit to within a foot of the hole. His tee shot was only twelve feet away from the cup but he had a tricky downhill putt which would not drop. I drove first on number seven and while he was teeing up his ball I said, "I like having the honor — it's better than following you — seeing those big booming drives of yours is enough to give anyone an inferiority complex." He just smiled a little, stuck to his concentration and crushed the ball up the middle about forty yards past mine. I misjudged the uphill distance to the green and my second shot went into the front trap. He needed only a pitching wedge for his second, but was very unhappy with the way he played the shot. The ball stayed on the green but far to the right of the hole — at least twenty-five feet — and I heard him let out a string of curse words. He did not like being one down and with that shot he may have blown an opportunity to get even. If I could just get down in two I would probably halve the hole because he would most likely two putt. My ball was sitting up in the sand about thirty-five feet from the pin. The green sloped upward and I wanted to hit the ball, with a lot of bite on it, about ten feet beyond the pin and have it draw back down the slope. I had a clear mental image of what I wanted to do and pulled it off. The ball spun backward almost hitting the pin and stopped four feet below. He had seen my sand shots on number one and number four and now with this one, which could have a real bearing on the match, he had to be impressed. He did not say anything and I did not look at him, but I knew that his eyes were on me so, as I smoothed out the sand, I put my hand to my mouth and yawned — as though a shot like that one were rather routine and tiresome. That broke him up. He laughed and was really amused, and it was a minute or so before he was able to collect himself and play his next stroke. He had a long side-hill putt which did not break as he had fig-ured and he left himself a very difficult above-the-hole three and a half footer. We were both lying three with fairly short but critical putts and it was possible for me to go two up, remain one up, or be even. I was away and although I hit the putt a little shakily, it went in. Now it was his turn and it was his putt, as much as anything else, that convinced me he was a real champion.

It was a delicate, curving, and hard-to-understand putt and would have to be struck with surgeon-like precision or it would not go in. A real good putter might make it once in six tries. He studied and stared at it from all angles, stealthily moving around in total concentration like a jungle cat stalking its prey. When he got into putting position, he stood over the ball for a few moments appearing to be in a trance, then tapped it so perfectly that its movement seemed to be still under his control and it disappeared into the cup. It was a marvelous moment but all I could say to him was "Bravo." I knew that putt could no more miss going in than the moon could move out of its orbit.

We moved on to the next hole in silence, an indication of one way in which we were alike. We believed that golf should be played as a contest with concentration and competition so keen that it was not possible to think of anything else. To relax or talk of other things would detract from the game. We were deeply in this match but, at the same time, I was preoccupied with wanting to know who he really was, but as long as we were playing there would be no opportunity to find out. Perhaps when we finished the first nine we could stop for a sandwich and a drink and that would give me the chance I wanted. The trouble with that was that I had to depend upon him to suggest it. Since I was not a member and was here as a guest of someone else, I could hardly do the inviting in a no-cash situation. He was the member, I was sure, and would suggest it.

My one-up position was still intact as we teed off on number eight. I played a very poor second shot but it turned out to be a "good miss" and reached the edge of the green about forty-five feet from the pin. His second shot was struck with the usual authority and stopped ten feet from the hole. The thing I had to do now was to try to get this first putt as close to the hole as possible to then make a par four so he would have to sink his putt in order to win the hole. "Anything can happen" happened — my first putt went in. It was so unexpected that I lost control of myself and went wild for a minute. He just stood there shaking his head slowly from side to side in utter disbelief. This was the first time that dumb luck had become a factor in the match, but what a factor and what a time — unless he made his putt he would go two down when a minute before it looked like the match could very well be even. Again he was faced with a "must-make" putt just to stay one down and again he went about it in his champion's way. His concentration became intense, evidenced by the way he glared at the ball and its line to the cup. I was sure that he would make it and he did.

The ninth hole was the longest on the course and, as expected, the Rolls Royce effectively outperformed the Chevrolet. He was on the apron of the 530-yard par five in two, and two putted for a birdie. I was on the green in three, and two putted. So at the halfway point the match was even. I shot 33, three under par; he was four under for the seven holes he played. When we got into the cart and started moving he said something about how much he was enjoying the match and my company, and as we neared a cartpath intersection he pointed to the left and said, "The tenth hole is this way." I had intended to turn to the right toward the clubhouse, but now that was out. Damn, I thought to myself, there goes the sandwich, the drink, and, most of all, my chance to get some information. Now I would have to wait until we finished the back nine.

When we drove up to the tenth tee, two other carts were already there and four men were standing on the tee. This foursome had played the front nine well ahead of us and evidently had stopped for a break and now were ready to go again. I remembered noticing these men on two occasions when the hole they were playing was close to where we were and they interrupted their play long enough to watch the shots we were about to make — or at least it seemed that way to me. We remained seated and then one of them looked at me and said, "You can play through if you like." I thanked him and both of us bounced out of the cart. Bob Clara moved quickly to the tee and hit a tremendous drive. I had become used to seeing him hit and did not say anything. But I could not believe that these men would not break out in some kind of spontaneous reaction to such a sight. But they did not — not one of them said a word — like they had not witnessed anything. And then I was again shocked when they complimented me on my drive, which was all right but not nearly the caliber of his. Something was mighty strange here. As we drove away I was about to ask him for an explanation, but then it occurred to me that if he knew them and they knew him, and because of that, acted with such total mutual indifference, the explanation might be something of considerable and unfavorable significance or embarrassment, so I decided to let it go. It was not likely that any other players would be out ahead of us on such a gloomy day.

We halved the tenth hole with par fours and the eleventh with par threes. I was playing extremely well — swinging confidently and with unusual smoothness from start to finish, and my putting stroke, which comes and goes, was definitely with me today. I could see no reason why I would not continue to play at my peak for the rest of the match, and while I could not seriously expect to win it, Bob Clara would know that he had been in a dogfight. But it is when you start thinking one way that things often start going another way.

It was not until we reached the twelfth tee that I realized the back nine was situated on higher ground than the front nine. Now, when I looked down the fairway, or in any other direction for that matter, much more of the East Lake landscape came into view than had been the case before. Perhaps it was the improved peripheral vision of distant vistas which caused the focus of my attention to blur temporarily. I had been so fascinated with the play of Bob Clara and the closeness of my match with him that now I was beginning to think that I was not fully appreciating the special qualities of the course itself, which to begin with, was my main reason for being here. So I tried to recapture and exploit the feeling which had taken hold of me the first time I saw East Lake.

How stupid I was. It did not work and I should have known that it would not. No one can make things like that happen — you just accept them on their terms, thankfully, if they come to you at all. It was just a short time that I had been out-of-tune, but long enough to have played the twelfth hole. I lost the hole, making the first bogie of the day and going one down for the first time. But on the thirteenth hole my head was clear again and I tore into the tee shot like a liberated tiger. "Well, welcome back," said Bob Clara, "Where have you been?" For a moment I thought of attempting a real answer, but then I decided, no way. Instead I said, "It's a habit of mine to fall asleep for two or three holes on the back side. I ruin more good rounds that way. But I'm telling you that today I have limited my nap to that one hole." He said, "I'm one up." I said, "There you go."

The thirteenth hole was a 384-yard par four and I

needed only a seven iron for my second shot, which I hit ten feet from the cup. While he was preparing to hit his second shot, my thinking started to race ahead and I figured that I had to win this hole or the fourteenth to stay in the match. The fifteenth and sixteenth were both par five holes, each a little more than 500 yards in length, and chances were that he would birdie both of them. If he were still one up after the fourteenth, the match could very well end at the sixteenth, with his margin of victory being 3 up and 2 to play. While I was visualizing all of that, he played a great pitching wedge to the green, stopping the ball less than a foot from the hole. His putt was so short that I had to concede it and now I had to make a ten-footer just to remain one down. There was no way I could afford to go two down. I looked the putt over very carefully and then struck the ball solidly into the center of the cup. I was still one down after the fourteenth, which was halved in par fours.

At this point the pace at which we were playing came to a halt for several minutes. We were in no hurry to leave the fourteenth green. It may have been that I felt the need for a breather before taking on those par fives. But a more likely reason was that from this spot we had an irresistible view of much of the East Lake course, the lake and the clubhouse as well. In addition to all of that which lay below us in the foreground, we could also see on the horizon that the promised change in weather, the cold front, was indeed coming. Dark clouds had covered the sky but now a great horizontal band of brightness appeared, growing and moving toward us as though a gigantic shade was being drawn back across the heavens. The land was being flooded with the oncoming light and it was a majestic sight. We sat there in the cart and watched the approaching light illuminate everything, including the far reaches of the course, and as it continued onto the lake and the clubhouse Bob Clara was moved to say, " . . . this little world . . . this blessed plot . . . this earth . . . this realm . . . this East Lake . . . ." "Well," I said, "Very good — how clever of you to have the Bard say it for us." Then we felt the wind and the sudden change in temperature. I started the cart and we drove to the fifteenth tee.

From here on the wind would be an important factor in our play. Strong and gusty, it would enter our thinking before every shot and putt. We would have a tail wind on fifteen, a head wind on sixteen, a cross wind on seventeen, and a head wind on eighteen. But concern for the wind could not have been the reason for the change which had come over Bob Clara. He tried not to show it, but I knew that something important was very much on his mind now. Whatever it was it did not affect his play to my advantage; in fact, his concentration seemed to intensify and he played like he had to dispose of me in a hurry, not just win. He had been the most considerate and mannerly person I had ever played golf with, and still was, in spite of whatever it was that was troubling him. He did not say anything but I got the feeling that he had remembered some urgent thing. Perhaps he realized that he was supposed to be somewhere else now or within a very short time.

He wasted no time hitting his tee shot on fifteen. I noticed that he teed the ball a little higher than usual, opened the club face, and hit the ball hard and high down wind. The ball carried so far that he needed only a four iron for his second shot, which he put on the green. I was within half a nine iron of the green after hitting two wood shots and then I knocked the ball stiff. He got down in two putts and I made my two-footer, halving the hole with a birdie four. But I could not do it again on the sixteenth. I did manage to make a par five despite the wind and thereby made him earn his win and two-up position. He birdied the sixteenth all right. He hit two wood shots against that strong wind and reached the edge of the putting surface. I would not have believed it possible and I don't know how the ball could stand being hit so hard. It is not often that a Rolls Royce has need or opportunity to display its amazing power, but it is there.

I was two down with two holes to play, still alive but barely. It would be all over if I lost or even halved the seventeenth. I had to win it to keep the match from ending. Bob Clara did not say he was two up. He did not say anything, nor did I. He hit another super drive which started out on the left side and by the time it came down the wind had moved it over to the middle of the fairway, about 140 yards from the green. I must have lost my concentration for a moment, rushed the swing, and hit a poor drive into the rough on the left side. The lie was not good enough to attempt hitting a wood club even though the distance to the green called for it. The green was sort of crescent-shaped with the pin on the top end, which was to the left. Most of the green was to the right and short of where the pin was. A deep crescent-shaped sand trap ran parallel to the green on the left side. I took the two iron from the bag, concentrated on making a good swing, and did make solid contact with the ball. The shot felt as good as any I had ever hit and the ball carried onto the green, stopping about thirty-five feet from the cup. I could very easily have failed in that situation, but I did not come apart, and Bob Clara rewarded me with a friendly grin and a casual salute, as if to say, "Well done." He also seemed to be thinking that this match is not over yet.

If my ball had not reached the green, I believe he would have quickly played his second shot into the fat part of the putting surface below the pin and settled for a par four which would either win or halve the hole for him, ending the match. But my ball was on the green and that gave him pause, and he took some time to think. He may have thought to himself that I might get "unconscious" again and sink that long putt like I did the one on number eight. At last it appeared that he had made up his mind and had decided to go for the pin — probably concluding that he had to be inside my ball and have a putt for a birdie three in case I made mine. But the shot he was going to attempt was extremely tough: there was very little putting surface to hit to around the pin; the wind would make club selection difficult; and the consequences for a less-than-perfect shot could be extremely unfortunate. Having made that first decision, he now had to decide how to play the shot. I figured that he could use an eight iron, nine iron, or pitching wedge, depending upon just what he intended to do.

He had taken time to plan the shot but then executed it without delay. He hit the nine iron high and to the left. The wind did not seem to affect the ball while it was rising but when it started down it drifted to the right, appearing as if it would fall in perfect alignment with the flag. Near the end of its descent, a strong buffeting gust of air pushed the ball back toward us and it dropped short of the green, hit the steep bank between the green and the trap, and kicked down onto the sand.

"Anything can happen" was happening again. He sat down heavily on the cart and as we rode I told him that it was the worst bit of luck I had ever seen. He looked bewildered and did not seem to notice that I had said anything. Whatever it was that had been bothering him the last few holes was worse now. In no way could it have been worry over the eventual outcome of the match. After all, he was the better player by far, he was still two up, and even if he were to lose this hole he would still be one up and only one to play. And, of course, we were not playing for the U.S. Open title. It had to be, as I had guessed before, that he had remembered some urgent thing requiring him to be somewhere else, but his time was running out and I was still hanging in there.

I stayed on the cartpath until we had gone around to the back of the green and parked about thirty yards from the eighteenth tee, which was just beyond some pine trees. I took my putter and he took his putter and sand wedge and we walked back to finish the seventeenth hole. The sand trap he was in, like all the others today, was perfectly smooth. From end to end the sand was completely free of foot prints or any other markings — the way sand at an ocean beach is after high tide. However, the last half hour of sun and wind had dried the surface sand and, although Bob Clara played a good shot, the ball came out of the sand more easily than he thought it would and it skipped past the pin about twelve feet. While he was smoothing the sand he had disturbed I had time to line up my thirty-five foot putt and was ready to go. I wanted to get this first one close and I did. The ball stopped even with the hole and just ten inches to the left, and rather than mark the ball I tapped it in for a par four. He was lying three and if he made his putt the match would be over. He studied it with the same intense concentration that he had shown on number seven and number eight holes and then he struck his putt just as perfectly as he had those. I was sure the ball was going in and so was he. It was rolling perfectly and straight for the cup — it could not miss. But somehow it did not go in. It stayed out, appearing to have been prevented from going in by some invisible barrier which guided it to the left, an inch past the hole. I could not believe what I had seen, and when I turned to him, the look that came into his staring eyes revealed that he was much more troubled by the *why* of the ball not going in than he was by the *fact* of it. I could see that he was fumbling, fearfully, and that something within him was going out of control. But then he regained his composure, partly for my sake I believe, and said that he hoped he had not upset me and asked that I go on ahead. I assumed that he meant to stay there alone for a minute or so, and perhaps try that putt again a time or two, before continuing with the match. I was going to ask if there was anything I could do for him, but he was trying so hard to hide the problem from me that I thought it better not to.

As I moved on alone to the eighteenth tee my thoughts were mixed, to say the least. I felt good about still being alive in the match. Being one down and one to play against such a formidable opponent was praiseworthy indeed. But I felt bad about Bob Clara's problem and the effect it was having on him. Everything had been great through fourteen holes;

then suddenly this change came over him. Why? Of course, I had no knowledge or understanding of what was causing his mental state but if, as I suspected, he remembered some other pressing engagement, why didn't he just tell me so and leave? That would have been a disappointment for both of us, but it would have been better than his suffering the way he was now. Or, having made the decision to continue to play despite the other pressing engagement, why could he not just make the best of it now and worry about the consequences later? Maybe he remembered when it was already too late to do anything about it, but could not help dreading the consequences. Maybe that last putt was some kind of omen. Maybe the cutting edge of the cold front which came through after we played the fourteenth hole had something to do with all of this. Maybe it would be better if I just stopped thinking about it.

The eighteenth hole was a 230-yard par three. We would be hitting into the teeth of the wind which was howling now. I had the honor, for the first time on the back side, and I teed the ball up knowing that I would be using the driver. It would take my best shot, and then some, to reach the green today. I was ready to play but my opponent was not yet here, so I waited. After a little while he had still not come, and I reasoned that the sympathy I felt for him should not include standing around in the cold unnecessarily. So I walked back to the seventeenth green to see what was going on. He was not there — he was not anywhere to be seen. My first thought was that he must have walked down the cartpath to the eighteenth tee just as I was walking the other way through the pine trees and we missed each other. So I immediately walked back to the eighteenth tee but he was not there. The cart was where I had left it, but now I noticed that his golf bag was no longer strapped to it. At this point I was only puzzled, not alarmed. I looked around in all directions and saw no one, so I got into the cart and drove back to the seventeenth green. There was still nothing to be seen and I stayed there for a while, dumbfounded. Then I noticed two moving carts about two hundred yards away. The four men who had let us play through were now headed toward the fifteenth tee. I caught up to them before they started to tee off. As I approached, one of the four spoke first, asking, "How's it going?"

I said, "O.K., but have you seen my playing partner?"

All four of them looked at me with blank expressions and then looked at each other. The one who had spoken before said, "Playing partner?"

"Yes," I said, "the fellow who was with me when you let us play through back on the tenth hole."

Again there was a pause and questioning glances exchanged among them. The same one spoke again and said, "You are the only golfer we have seen out here today, other than ourselves."

I said nothing more and all of us remained as we were for several seconds. I began to feel something strange happen inside my body — like the pull of gravity had suddenly been greatly increased and was dragging on my insides. I remember looking at my fingernails to see if the flesh underneath had become blue. (During the war we made this simple test to check for shock or oxygen loss, and I did it now automatically.) Then I must have started to shake and tremble because two of the men rushed toward me as if to assist me. But I caught hold of myself and the violence of the sensation subsided. I told them that I would be all right now, and left. I got back onto the path which took me past the seventeenth green and the eighteenth tee, and as I continued on, I noticed a man standing alone near the last green. Closer now, I could see that he was my host, the stockbroker. He left work early and stopped here on his way home to see how I liked the course. When he saw my face he said, "What is the matter?" I was not able to say anything yet and he said, "I was inside a minute ago and they told me that some new guy was out here playing alone and really tearing the course apart. I figured it was you."

"I played very well," I told him, "but I was not alone. I started out alone but I met a fellow on the third tee and he and I played together through the seventeenth hole and now he's disappeared. He must be the best golfer in the world."

"Come on inside and have a drink," the member said. "I want to hear about this — and I want Doc Cameron to hear it too." Doc Cameron was introduced to me as being East Lake's oldest and best member. He was a fine old gentleman and a lifelong member of the club. He could not play golf anymore, but came out to the course almost every day to talk golf with the players and drink scotch. He especially loved to tell about the long-ago experiences which remained in his memory.

I told them everything — starting with my love for the game which brought me out to East Lake in the first place, and ending with my conversation with the foursome a little while ago. I gave an almost stroke-by-stroke account of what had gone on, and I included facts of special significance relating to Bob Clara's play, as well as my thoughts and opinions concerning his character and personality. They listened most intently and interrupted only occasionally to ask for clarification of some particular thing. When I finished, we sat there for a while without anything being said. Then my host said, "Doc, what do you make of it?"

Doc Cameron lifted his glass to his lips and swallowed what was left in it. Another round was ordered (the third) and then he said, "There's only one thing that I'm sure of, and that is who the other player was." He looked me square in the eyes and said, "You played that match with Bob Jones."

"Bob Jones," I murmured.

"Yes," he said. "Of course, the world knew him as Bobby Jones, but he was never called that around here. His family and friends always called him Bob, never Bobby. He hated to be called Bobby."

Somehow I knew he was right, but I said, "How the hell could I have played golf today with Bobby Jones?"

"I don't know how," he said, "but I am more sure of that than I am of anything. From the very beginning — when you were on the third and fourth holes — I knew that it was Jones, and everything else you said afterward just confirmed it. That was Bob Jones you played golf with today — or his ghost."

"Wait a minute," I said, "let's consider the facts and examine this thing rationally. One, Bobby Jones — I mean Bob Jones — was born in 1902 and died in 1971. If he were still living he would be eighty years old on his next birthday. Obviously, I did not play with that Bob Jones. Two, the person I played with could not have been a ghost; ghosts are not real — they are spirits and don't have bodies. I shook hands with this man and I could feel his weight when he got in and out of the cart, etc. Believe me, he was real."

My host said, "How do you account for the other people in the foursome not seeing him?"

"I can't account for that," I said.

"Did Bob Clara leave anything of his in the cart, like a golf ball, a sweater, a head cover, or anything?" he asked.

I had to answer "No" to that. Then I remembered something I wanted to ask Doc Cameron before but had forgotten. So I turned to him and said, "Why would Bob Jones tell me his name was Bob Clara?"

Doc Cameron smiled a little, and said, "Yeah, I've thought of that too — all I can tell you is that Bob Jones' mother's name was Clara, one of his two daughters was named Clara, and when Jones was a little boy he named his pony Clara." There was no more conversation concerning the name.

Then a thought came to me and I asked both men, "Could a ghost leave footprints in a sand trap?" Both heads shook "No." I said, "Doc, you wait here, we'll be back in a few minutes," and I motioned for my host to come with me. We went outside and the cart with my bag on it was still there. "Come on," I said, "We're taking a little ride." On the way I told him what the traps were like today, that I had been in several but that Bob Jones had been in only one — at the seventeenth green. I said that I would show him just where his ball had been in the trap and, while Jones had smoothed out the sand after hitting his shot, we would most certainly be able to tell whether a shot had been played from the spot. We left the cart on the path and walked down around to the side of the trap away from the green. It had started to get a little dark outside by now, but there was still more than enough light to see that the entire trap had not been touched. It could not have been more evident that nobody had set foot on that sand today. We rode back to the club-house and my friend explained to Doc Cameron the what, where, and why of our absence.

After another drink and a long period of silence I said, "What kind of trouble do you suppose ghosts can get into? Bob Jones was certainly stewing about something. I hope I didn't cause his problem. Do you suppose spirits have laws and rules they have to abide by? I wonder who it is that they have to report to." My two drinking partners did not show any interest in pursuing this kind of talk. In fact, Doc Cameron looked like he was thinking of something else. He said, "In the summer of 1930, I played a round here with Bob Jones. It was just a few days before he left for Philadelphia to play in the United States Amateur and he was trying to keep his game tuned up. He shot a sixty-three that day and went on to Merion and won the Amateur, completing his famous Grand Slam. Man, was he ever ready to play."

I got the feeling that Doc was just getting started and could go on all night. Perhaps some other time I would really enjoy hearing him, but not now. I had to get away soon. The two of them were really relaxed now, and I did not get much response when I said that I had to leave. So I stood up, and while that was a mild surprise for them, it did not cause them to move. I thanked them, said how much I enjoyed being in their company, and I told my host that I would call him. They wished me well. At the door, a young fellow was waiting to help me with my golf gear.

It was almost dark outside, but the weather was beautiful. The air was crisp, bracing, and clear as a bell and the East horizon was aglow, brightened by a harvest moon rising beneath. The evening was something to be thankful for, as was the entire day, a day for which I felt most privileged and grateful as well as astonished. I accepted what the day had brought, trauma and all. The match with Bobby Jones was the golf highlight of my life. I thought again about that problem of his — but what I thought was — how could he possibly have a problem now? The ways of fate are strange — was the problem really mine and not his, as it had appeared? I drove slowly along the driveway and through the gate, and when I had left the grounds there no longer seemed reason to worry, but all of my life I would wonder.

Ted Ray, who came to East Lake in 1913 and hit what Bobby
Jones called "the greatest shot I ever saw."

Four teenagers raise the flag at the dedication of the new clubhouse at East Lake in 1917. Left to right: Mariana Goldsmith,
Virginia Ashe, Douglass Paine, and Margaret Rogers.

Bobby Jones at age twenty, six months after his record 63 at East
Lake and three months before his first national championship, the
1923 U.S. Open at Inwood.

Joyce Wethered, who possessed the swing Bobby called "the most perfect in the world."

Bobby Jones (left) and Watts Gunn at the U.S. Amateur at Oakmont in 1925. It was, and still is, the only time two members of the same club have met in the final of that tournament.

"Long Jim" Barnes after winning the British Open in 1925. He defeated seventeen-year-old Bobby Jones in the first Southern Open at East Lake in 1919 with his eagle three on the fifth hole.

Charlie Yates at St. Andrews in 1938, just before leading the
crowd in "A Wee Deoch and Doris."

To Pierre
with warm regards
from his partner
Charlie

Bobby Jones shows the new British Amateur champion,
Charlie Yates, how to grip *Calamity Jane* (1938).

Charlie Harrison receives an Atlanta Athletic Club trophy from Bobby Jones in 1945.

Tommy Barnes checks the scorecard while Bobby and friends look on—at the end of what was to be Bobby's last round on August 18, 1948. Also shown are Robert Ingram and Henry Linder.

Bobby Jones listens to his friend, Robert W. Woodruff. Imagined quote: "Bob, I want to tell you my favorite Bobby Jones story. When I played St. Andrews, I had this caddie who said very little . . ."

A picture of every father's dream—winning our flight when our son wins the championship. Jim and Charles Harrison at East Lake.

Tommy Barnes at age seventy-seven, with the author at East Lake in 1992.

Charlie Elliott relaxing at home in 1994. He was a longtime golfing friend of Bobby Jones and his favorite hunting and fishing companion.

Jim Gerber, Director of Golf at East Lake, with Charlie Yates in 1995.

Tom Cousins and Charlie Yates during the renovation of the clubhouse of the new East Lake Golf Club (1995).

Ann and Tom Cousins. Two golfers who brought East Lake back to life—for all of us.

The Clubhouse at East Lake

VI

BACK TO THE PRESENT

$\mathcal{T}$he trees at East Lake give the course much of its character. Mature catalpas line the first fairway and huge white pines and mature dogwoods are every-where.[17] Beauty is not their only purpose; on several holes big trees influence shot planning. For instance, on number six a big oak may come into play when the tee is on the left, and from the back tees on sixteen a tall tree may bother a drive hit right to left. Also, the drive on seventeen can be affected by a tree on the left side of the fairway. One friendly feature of the trees is that the lower branches are pruned so a full swing can be taken even if a ball lies directly under — similar to Augusta National. Some trees give other pleasures. In summer a mulberry sprinkles its fruit over the third tee

---

[17] The catalpas offer more than shade and beauty. Charlie Harrison knows that Bobby and Charlie Elliott liked to use the "worms" from the trees to fish in the lake.

The white pines at East Lake give the golfer the impression that he's playing golf far-ther north. The species doesn't usually flourish so far south, but at East Lake they can figure in every hole.

and in late fall golfers enjoy pecans at the first tee.

Spring at East Lake unfolds over several months. In February, the first color appears in the red maples, like those which line the driveway and the one behind the fifth green. In March, all of the oaks, hickories, and other hardwoods bloom. White dogwoods dominate in April; then in May, just when you think it's all over, the huge catalpas open up with fragrant, white orchid-like flowers and a thousand magnolia blossoms send their heavy lemon scent into the air.

It also takes time for the zoysia fairways and Bermuda rough to turn. Bright green shoots appear in February, but the winter brown isn't gone until May. In between, there is pleasure in watching the process — a patchwork of green and brown which varies with slope and exposure. The contrast between the zoysia and Bermuda is especially beautiful in the early morning. Dew sits up on the grass of the rough, but the water droplets slide down the thicker blades of the zoysia. The contrast is so striking that it looks like the fairways have been mowed during the night.

Because of all the mature hardwoods, fall colors are special, especially considering how far south we are. But many golfers like the winter best since everything is wide open, and they know that their friends up north have put their clubs away and are waiting for their favorite courses to open back up in March or April.

One hundred and eighty acres looks at a big section of sky. The close-in location east of town puts the golf course in a good position several miles from a busy airport, but the planes aren't constant and don't intrude. They fly at a pleasant height and entertain those on the ground. Golfers usually pay attention to events below and unless their minds are wandering, don't look up when they hear a familiar sound, like an airplane near a big city. But when something unusual happens up there, it breaks into the mind, even if the sound is distant.

The honking of Canada geese is such a sound, and heads pop up and fingers point when they go by at medium height. But one bright day in late February of 1992 on the eighteenth, member Brem Mayer called attention to an even more unusual sound. It was the voice of the sandhill crane migrating back to Michigan and Manitoba. That day, a flock of fifty or sixty seemed confused and aimless as they spiralled straight up, clamoring at each other. The foursome froze. Finally, when they were almost out of sight, at least five times as high as the geese, they found the breeze they wanted, formed themselves into a shallow vee, and slowly moved away to the northwest. It was an awesome sight, and a wild and haunting sound.

Long before the lake and golf course, the red-tailed hawk was master of the land at East Lake. For millions of years this colorful bird has soared high over the pines and oaks, just as he does today. One day he gave golfers a thrill by gliding close by at four feet. He used the rolling ground as a blind and suddenly pounced on his prey. He loves to fan his rust-colored tail at us as he takes his perch in a tree on the other side of the fairway. No round at East Lake is complete unless visited by the hawk. Golfers glory in his presence. He reminds us of ourselves as we fight our own battles below.

Smaller birds are constant company at East Lake. Ducks, killdeer, and red-wing blackbirds are always there, and beautiful herons and egrets frequently visit.

The lake is another treasure. Some people have lake houses one or two hours away that require work and worry to get ready. East Lake gives all of the pleasure of a country get-away — but it's right here, 10-20 minutes away from home or work, right in town. Also, this lake house is always full of friends and a friendly staff who are ready with wonderful refreshments, outstanding food, and smiles all around.

For the golfer, the lake may not always be an advantage, but it adds a lot of interest. After a downpour dumped three inches of rain on the property in a few hours in November of 1992, member Dick Boyens went out to look around: "I've never seen the water so high. Only the putting surface was above water on number six. The bunkers were flooded and full of jumping fish. I've never seen that before." East Lake appeared in 1892, when Doolittle Creek was dammed up. It is fed by seven springs, is twenty-seven acres in area, and has an average depth of thirteen feet.

Like the great links courses in England and Scotland, East Lake is an ideal walking course. Only the hill up fifteen is a bit tiring — the rest are gentle. It's the least hilly course in Atlanta, but there are no dull flat holes — there's plenty of movement in the fairways and subtle break in the greens.

In a 1992 article on Muirfield in *Golf Magazine*, Tom Weiskopf wrote: "The course is not repetitious . . . is entirely in front of you . . . very little is hidden from view . . . no tricks." All of that fits East Lake perfectly. Except for one hole, the fifteenth, the greens can be seen from the tees. This allows planning and gives instant feedback, anxiety reducing features that make every round therapeutic, like a long gentle massage.

Bobby Jones never liked blind shots, probably because of where he grew up. At the height of his fame he visited a course just north of New York City. When the members who had invited him asked him about the course, he smiled and said: "I had a great time and it's a wonderful course, but there are lots of blind shots." That summer, bulldozers arrived to change five or six holes. It may be that the reason he rarely made casual comments is that they were usually taken seriously, and could cause expense or inconvenience to others.

East Lake is better known than most members think. One recently found himself in Scotland with some time on his hands. He took a train to Troon and

looked up the famous Royal Troon Golf Club. He found
the secretary seated in the hall looking down at the pair-
ing sheets and meekly announced: "I'm from East Lake
in Atlanta, Georgia, in the States, and would love to play
Old Troon. Any chance?" . . . Silence . . . still looking
over the pages on the table. Again, after a minute or
two: "That's the home course of Bobby Jones." The
head rose wearily: "Good God, man. I know that. What
do you take me for, a bloody idiot? I'm going to find a
member to take you out. Try to be patient."

All of the older members have their own memories
of Bobby Jones. They tell of the warmth of his personality, his self-deprecating sense of humor, the deep
belly laugh, and his keen mind. Also, it's easy for them
to remember his swing with its remarkable rhythm
and full turn.[18] However, for those of us who have
come later and never knew him, Charlie Yates, Charlie
Elliott, and Tommy Barnes are the best links that
remain to connect us to Bobby Jones.*

Time spent with Charlie Yates today is as close as
we can come to visiting with Bobby Jones. His greatest pleasure, like his late friend, is relaxing with his
family and a few good friends. Like Bobby, he is the
essence of the Southern Gentleman, preferring to do
his good works privately to enrich his city and its peo-

---

[18] Roger Cordes compared Bobby's use of language to his golf: "His speech was a lot
like his swing, nothing was wasted; every word and every movement was there for a
purpose."
* Charlie Elliott is Georgia's "naturalist emeritus." The new Charlie Elliott Wildlife
Center near Monticello testifies to that. His memories of Jones are recorded in "My
Love Affair with East Lake."

ple. Also, you have to work hard to get him to talk about himself; he always wants to talk about you.

Only a few Atlantans know that as head of the Atlanta Arts Alliance, he was a driving force behind the emergence of the Atlanta Symphony and personally brought Robert Shaw to Atlanta to start our musical excellence. Also, very few know that he is one of the men responsible for the Robert T. Jones, Jr. Scholarship which exchanges students between Emory University in Atlanta and St. Andrews in Scotland. Like his famous older friend, Charlie Yates is one of Atlanta's treasures.

He has Bobby's ability to make those with him the center of attention and his eyes light up and twinkle with humor when he tells some wonderful story with his perfect memory and timing. But he differs from his friend in two ways. Up in front of a crowd he seems like a professional storyteller, and he especially loves introducing friends in the audience to everyone else, always adding a humorous sentence or two to relax the people he points out. By all accounts, Bobby Jones was genuinely modest and retiring in public, but Charlie is at his best up on the stage, working the crowd.[19] Secondly, Charlie Yates, like Col. Jones but not like Bobby, loves to sing. He'll open up into song on the slightest provocation. Witnesses who were at St. Andrews in 1938 love to tell about Charlie, stand-

---

[19] Bobby confided to Charlie one day while riding to Augusta from Atlanta, "I really like people, but I like 'em in small doses." He must have loved and appreciated good conversation between a few people in private more than oratory and big crowds.

ing with his back to the clubhouse, leading several hundred Scots in "A Wee Deoch and Doris." He will sing it for you today. All you have to do is ask.

That singing session occurred after Charlie's team had just lost the Walker Cup. Nineteen-thirty-eight was also the year of his British Amateur victory at Troon, but he didn't lead a crowd in song at his own moment of triumph. For a man with Charlie's values, such a display would have been ungentlemanly.

Like Bobby Jones, in Atlanta and in Britain, Charlie is loved more for his behavior than for what he has accomplished. In *Golf Between Two Wars*, Bernard Darwin wrote, " . . . he hit the ball straight and far and he was a sure and beautiful putter . . . There has been no invading Champion more popular than Charlie Yates, whose cheerfulness and humour, of his own particular brand, made everybody like him." At the British Amateur at Hoylake in 1995, he was asked to sing again, and as usual he obliged his friends; they will never forget the way he acted when his side lost in 1938.

In 1976, Herbert Warren Wind interviewed Charlie after a presentation about Bobby at the Memorial Arts Center. The program was part of the festivities surrounding the playing of the U.S. Open at the new course of the Atlanta Athletic Club. One month before his death, in a letter in November 1971, Bobby had requested that the United States Golf Association bring the event to "my home club." The brief interview tells us a lot about our heritage at East Lake and a little about our "President Charlie."

In a July 1976 issue of *The New Yorker*, Wind wrote:

Some of us then adjourned to a small dining room in the Center for refreshment and conversation. I spotted Yates free in a corner, and hurrying over, congratulated him on how well the tribute had gone. As I was doing this, I suddenly realized that, while I have known Yates for a good many years, I had never asked him about his friendship with Jones. 'You must remember that there was quite a gulf in years between Bob and me — eleven years,' he said. 'I knew him pretty well, though, I think. My family, beginning with my grandfather, had a summer place out at East Lake, so when I wasn't playing golf myself I'd follow Bob and watch him play. He was awfully nice to kids like me. From time to time, he'd give me a golf ball — not an old beat-up one but a nice, pretty ball. Or when he saw you in the clubhouse he'd wave you over and buy you a Coke. I can't tell you how much he meant to us all. I still remember hearing on the radio the special bulletin that he had won our 1930 Amateur, the last trick in the Grand Slam. I was so excited that I ran from our house to the clubhouse yelling to everyone I saw on the course, 'Bobby's won! Bobby's won!' I have so many fond memories of East Lake. You know I love to sing — I have what is referred to as a locker-room tenor — and I particularly loved to sing in the showers with Bob's dad, the Colonel. He had a big, bellowing bass voice. Our specialties were 'Lonesome Road,' 'Ol' Man River,' and 'Home on the Range.' On that last one, we'd really shake the timbers.'

In the 1930's, Tommy Barnes spent hours trying to copy the swing of his famous older friend. Although the stance and swing are different, it's pleasant now, while watching Tommy, to think about the first edition. Tommy is 82 years old and, standing still, he looks like it might be true. But he moves and plays like a man in his fifties — he's a biological marvel. Like Bobby, he plays so fast that you have to keep watching or you'll miss his shot. He never uses a practice swing. After he takes his stance, the feet move two or three times and the clubhead waggles back and forth as he checks the target. Then he settles down to the ball. That's when it starts, slow and graceful and still working perfectly, as predictable and lazy as an old oil well, slowly rocking as it pumps. The shoulder turn is full and the weight shifts smoothly back and through the ball. The left knee comes in, the right moves out, and everything seems to be in fluid motion, until you notice the head and eyes. They are fixed, rigid and stable while surrounded by motion, until made to move—to follow the body through the ball. The usual result is a slight draw of medium height, perfectly suited to his favorite course.

A round of golf on any course with Tommy Barnes is an experience to be treasured. He's in constant motion, except when someone else is standing over a shot. If a feeble older guest is faced with an uneven teeing area, he'll grab the tee markers and move them to a better spot. He is a natural teacher. When paired with a struggling mediocre golfer, he knows just what to say to help. He never says, "Don't sway." Instead he gives us something to do right: "Keep your head behind the ball." On the green, since he's usually closer, he seems to hold the flag for everyone else. He concedes a lot of putts but always putts his own, studying the line with a quick cock of the head before he settles down to business.

His motto is "think positive." One of his favorite partners over the years at East Lake was Pete Brown, the former Georgia Tech football player and good friend. Once, when paired with Tommy in the club championship, Pete was full of doubt; he had no confidence in his swing and seemed to think that fate was against him that day. Tommy talked with him several times trying to get him turned around. "Pete, no one can be successful in this game with negative thoughts; you've got to have a positive attitude." That seemed to help, but in a few more holes, Pete fell back into negative language and became upset. This went on throughout the round. Finally, on the last tee, Pete's confidence collapsed again. For about the tenth time, Tommy said, "Pete, you've just got to stop all that negative talk." Finally, a smile crossed Pete's face, "Don't worry, Tommy. I know I'm talking negative, but I'm thinking positive."

Before the renovation in 1994, he would ride his cart at East Lake all over the place, bouncing over to encourage his friends: "I wish I could play a shot like that!" He seemed to know everyone and he wanted them all to have as much fun as possible — he was their host. There was always time for a good story on the course and he loved being wherever he was at the moment, which made those with him feel important — the genius of the gentleman. He loved East Lake and taught others to do the same: "I've played a lot of the great courses in this country and never found another one I like as much. There's not a bad hole out here. It's a great golf course."

The memory of Bobby Jones lives today in the stories of his many friends around the world, and they will hand them down safely to their children and new friends. In Georgia, his friends still gather at the Atlanta Athletic Club, the Capital City Club, Peachtree Golf Club, and at Augusta National Golf Club, and they will keep his memory alive. But the 180 acres at East Lake will hold the memories best. The children and grandchildren of his friends will come here with their stories, to walk in his footsteps on his own land. They will think about how lucky they are to have listened to them, and to have remembered.

Back inside after a round, all members enjoy showing their guests the old double locker which says *ROBT. T. JONES*. It's still all here. This precious ground has been scarred by the irons of most of the greats of this century, including Vardon and Ray. When you come, come with appreciation for those who have come before, and tip your cap to the great Bobby Jones — his spirit still walks the grand fairways of old East Lake, sharing stories with his friends, and with us.

Number one is a 424-yard par four played into the prevailing breeze.

The second is a 192-yard par three over a pond. In 1908, this was the site of a summer home of the Jones family.

The third, a 387-yard par four — The fairway crosses the old Fayetteville Road.

The Alston House, one of the oldest in Atlanta, in 1996.

The fourth, a 440-yard par four — In 1913 Ted Ray's mashie-niblick cleared the top of a tree. Bobby Jones called it "the greatest shot I ever saw."

East Lake's hawk near the fourth green, turning toward home on the back nine.

The fifth, a 561-yard par five — Where "Long Jim" Barnes beat seventeen-year-old Bobby Jones with his amazing eagle three in 1919.

In February the first color appears in the red maples, like those along the driveway and the ones behind the fifth green.

The sixth, a 164-yard par three — Bobby said: "Use an old ball."

— painting by Gordon Wheeler in 1998.

Number seven, a 394-yard par four — On this hole Harvey
Penick saw Bobby Jones hit "the best golf shot I ever saw in
a tournament."

Eight, a 360-yard par four — It was a trench in the Civil War.

The ninth, a 584-yard par five — A beautiful view of the lake and clubhouse slowly develops as we leave the ninth tee. At this place, and at many others, the golfer seems to be walking in the park of an old English estate.

The ninth, looking back (May, 1998).

The 516-yard uphill par five tenth — Off to the left are the houses of Alexa Stirling and Watts Gunn, and Mrs. Meadow's boarding house, the starting point of five-year-old Bobby Jones' makeshift course along Daniel Avenue and Alston Drive.

In early spring (top), and in summer.

Number eleven, a 192-yard par three — To Arnold Palmer in 1963 it seemed to curve around a tree on the right: "I've never seen a dog-leg par three before."

Hawk's view of golf course construction in 1994, from high above the fifteenth fairway.

Twelve, a 391-yard par four — the golfer's first look at Atlanta's skyline.

There is drama at the end of this peaceful looking downhill par four.

Thirteen, a 400-yard par four — "We rushed out to my 1932
Pontiac and drove out to behind the thirteenth green."

Before the bunkers were filled, in 1994 — The contrast
between the zoysia and Bermuda is especially beautiful in
the early morning.

The fourteenth, a 442-yard par four — In 1935 Joyce Wethered outdrove Bobby Jones and Charlie Yates on this hole.

"Miss Wethered's Valley" — between the thirteenth tee and fourteenth green.

Fifteen, a 495-yard par five — the climax of the Colonel's most
unusual tournament.
"Preacher?" Colonel Bob roared. "Who's a preacher?"

Long before the lake and golf course the red-tailed hawk was
master of the land at East Lake.

Sixteen, a 481-yard par four — Pierce Harris said: "Charlie, we should have known that we could not compete today against such a combination of proficiency and profanity."

The view from the sixteenth green in winter.

The seventeenth is a 453-yard par four and a walk along the edge of the lake.

On September 16, 1922, twenty-year-old Bobby Jones sank a twenty foot birdie putt on the seventeenth and moved to nine under par.

About the eighteenth, a 232-yard par three, Colonel Jones said: ". . . that drive calls for all there is, in the delicatessen department."

On September 16, 1922: "Bobby drew the trusty old driving iron . . . and the little white sphere bored its way, upheld by the backspin, climbing, climbing — to drop lightly, just at the right of the green."

Alexa Stirling, the first East Lake golfer to win a national championship, and her house, renovated in 1998.

Assistant Jeff Lark with a group, waiting for the weather to let them start.

Jack Nicklaus, teaching at East Lake in 1998,

and with Wendy Roper, left, Tony Smith, Mike Rensink, Director of Golf Rick Burton, and Head Professional Chad Parker.

Jack Glenn, Jr. and Charles Steppes, III.

Fully loaded sophomore Eddie Davenport in 1998, standing where Ted Ray stood 85 years before.

"One shirt's in the dryer." Jon Migely and his charges on the ninth green.

John Beal, Sheralyn Feezell, and Matthew Whitaker.

Beate de Priest, with Bobby Jones' old double locker in the pro-shop.

Sam Puryear, on May 12, 1998, showing the new generation how to do it—*Golf With a Purpose.*

VII

INTO THE FUTURE–
GOLF WITH A PURPOSE

*L*ike Bobby Jones, those of us who were able to play golf with our parents remember how interesting it was to see them working to hit good shots. We loved it that our own rare good swings were praised and that our failures brought out sympathetic encouragement from those who were most important to us.

We remember what our dad's face and eyes looked like when he concentrated on a putt, and how he acted and what he said when he missed the one he wanted. We saw him speak to his friends and introduce strangers to each other. We saw how he shook hands and looked people in the eye. We watched and listened.

Young people flourish with support and structure and they watch us carefully.

This is one reason the restoration of the old golf course in 1994 was so important. It started the rebirth of the neighborhood and led to the formation of the New Community at East Lake, which is putting young people in Atlanta outside in the natural world, doing something difficult on their own, trying to make an honest score in a game that is a good model for the challenges that lie ahead in their lives.

The new public Charlie Yates Golf Course and surrounding community is taking shape in 1998 with after school mentoring of youngsters in self discipline and behavior. National and international corporations are leading the effort, since these business leaders know that the long term success of society depends upon the new generation.

At East Lake innovative housing patterns are already in place with space outdoors to invite children and their parents to enjoy time together after school and work, like Bobby and his parents almost a century ago. New community facilities are planned so healthy activities can continue even when weather won't let them out onto the golf course; and there will be educational advantages that did not exist before in the old tightly clustered public housing project that existed on the same site before.

Many successful adults learned the game as caddies, and the Western Golf Association offers college scholarships to those who wish to join their friends caddying on the famous older course next door. There they can form relationships with men and women they would not spend time with otherwise.

Charles Steppes, III and Jack Glenn, Jr. are good examples of the relationships that are there for the making, and one story tells how they began.

Jack is an example of P.G. Wodehouse's famous statement: "Golf is like measles and should be caught young; if contracted late in life the results can be serious."

In 1996 fourteen-year-old Charles was trying to learn the complex craft of caddying. He didn't know yet just where to stand, when to be still, or how to handle all the clubs. One day Jack was standing over a fifteen foot putt on the tenth green and Charles was holding the flag, hoping he was doing it right. Jack backed away from the important one dollar putt: "Charles, I want you to talk to this ball all the way to the hole. Strong language will not offend me if you think it will help." Finally off went the putt. "Com'on," said Charles, first softly, then when it seemed to lose its speed, "COM'ON!" and a mournful "AW!" as it stopped a foot short. We all smiled at each other, enjoying the moment; and one of us smiled more, saving the dollar.

Under his grandfather's expert eye Charles has become a golfer, but he still gets a kick out of Jack and his friends. Also, he understands our failures now, and smiles and gives us positive feedback when we do right, saying simply, "that's a great shot." We love it when we earn a young man's praise.

Relationships formed at East Lake across generations will not be limited to the golf course — contacts outside and supportive advice will continue if needed, long after golf rounds are done.

Does "Golf With a Purpose" mean that some young people will become successful professional golfers? Perhaps, but it's more important that they learn how to meet new people and set goals for themselves and accomplish them. Then they will grow up and help us solve our common problems.

This is a great time to come to East Lake and help it all happen.

VIII

Two Different
Meanings of East Lake

The Historical

*L*ike our oldest family members and friends, East Lake has lived as an institution in Atlanta for over ninety years — a life which has spanned our century. Its active, most successful period so far lasted sixty years, and during that time it produced an unusual succession of outstanding golfers and tournament victories.

The great Bobby Jones learned to play here and he grew up to win three regional and thirteen national golf championships. His career ended at the age of twenty-eight, with the Grand Slam of Golf in 1930, an achievement many rate as the greatest in the history of sports. In all, East Lake has given birth to twenty-one regional and twenty-one national golf champions. During this period, as part of the Atlanta Athletic

Club, East Lake was the Eden of three generations of Atlantans, as closely woven into their personal lives as their own homes.

East Lake then passed through twenty-five years in which the world seemed to forget. Many people who had loved it thought it had been destroyed. It was threatened from all sides.

Today, unlike our older human friends, East Lake has been restored to the physical condition of its youth, but it's even better now since it has the face and body of the young, but the memories and soul of a great-grandparent. In the last few years of the twentieth century East Lake is walking back onto the world stage, confident this time, not only because of its beauty, but because of its splendid history.

The Personal

No words ever written express a golfer's affection for his home course better than the way Bobby Jones chose to end *Down the Fairway* in 1927:

Sometimes I get to thinking, with a curious little sinking away down deep, how I will feel when my tournament days are over, and I read in the papers that the boys are gathering for the national open, or the amateur . . . Maybe at one of the courses I love so well, and where

I fought in the old days . . . It's going to be queer.

But there's always one thing to look forward to — the round with Dad and Chick and Brad; the Sunday morning round at old East Lake, with nothing to worry about, when championships are done.

ACKNOWLEDGEMENTS

*I*n the late 1960's, after the painful decision was finally made by the Atlanta Athletic Club to sell East Lake, a fateful second decision was made. Fired up with frustration, member Paul R. Grigsby decided to buy it back and protect it. He and his partners stood by during many difficult years. They preserved it for the world and deserve our eternal gratitude.

During the turmoil of the sixties, after Paul and his partners had bought the course and clubhouse, he met with Bobby Jones to discuss the fate of the property. Bobby reassured Paul about the future: "Don't worry, Paul, the Athletic Club is my club, but East Lake is my golf course."

In December of 1993, Atlantan Tom Cousins assumed ownership of East Lake and gave it to a foundation determined to restore the surrounding neighborhood. His association goes back a long way as his father was a prominent member during Bobby Jones' day. One day when Tom was thirteen years old, he was playing the front nine in the rain. He hit his second shot on the ninth hole into the water and had to take off his shoes to play his third. The ball came out, and the barefooted young golfer wound up with par 36 on nine holes for the first time. Bobby would have smiled to know it. East Lake is in good hands.

With thanks to his friends Watts Gunn,
Charlie Yates, Charlie Elliott,
Tommy Barnes, Cy Strickler, Richard Courts,
Harvey Hill, Gene Branch,
Marion and Ralph Williams, and
Mariana Goldsmith Eager;
and to Paul Grigsby and his partners;
and with appreciation for the editing of
Herbert Warren Wind, Floyd C. Watkins,
Lee Blinson, Rie Calcaterra, Melanie Smallie,
and Mary Zeliff;
and with affection for the wonderful
staff at East Lake;
and for golfing friends Brem, Anne, Jack,
Charlie, Peter, Wayne, Linton, Cam,
Laura, and Priscilla;
and with special thanks to Tom Cousins
for taking over when he was needed;
this book is dedicated to the memory of
Robert Tyre Jones, Jr.
(1902 - 1971)

APPENDIX

A WEE DEOCH AND DORIS

(contributed by Charlie Yates)

Verse: There's a good old Scottish custom
            That has stood the test of time.
            It's a custom that's been carried out
            In every land and clime.
            Where brother Scots foregather
            It's aye the usual thing
            Just before we say good nicht
            We fill our cups and sing:

Chorus: Just a wee deoch and doris*
            Just a wee drap, that's a',
            Just a wee deoch and doris
            Before we gang awa'.
            There's a wee wifie waiting
            In a wee but and ben.**
            But if you can say, "It's a braw bricht
                moonlicht nicht."†
            Well, ye're a' richt.†† ye Ken!

*   deoch and doris: A dram of whisky
**   but and ben: a two-roomed cottage
†   braw bricht moonlicht nicht: bright, moonlit night
††   Ye're a' richt: you're all right

WHAT GOLF MEANS TO ME

Linton C. Hopkins, Sr. [20]

c. 1915

To get a Wednesday afternoon for golf, I have to rush around in the office all morning, doing a whole day's work in half a day. When 12:30 comes, screwed up to about a thousands pressure to the square inch, I gallop downstairs to the lunch counter and swallow a pie and a cup of coffee. Grabbing my car, I beat it for the country club. In a few minutes, I develop a terrible indigestion. Usually, on the way, I get arrested for speeding. That causes delay, so when I get through arguing with the policeman I have to hurry faster than ever. At the club, I hurry out of my clothes. I usually tear my unions badly. I hurry out to the first tee. Then I try to calm down. I give myself auto-suggestions. I say: "I will relax. I will not hurry. I am not in a hurry. I'm very quiet and calm now." But inside I know I'm a terrible liar.

Then I start out. And I hittem in the rough; I hit-

---

[20] Linton C. Hopkins, Sr. (1872-1943) was an Atlanta attorney and mystery writer who was a contemporary of Bobby's father, Robert P. Jones. He was a longtime member of the Atlanta Athletic Club, and he taught his five children (Nina, John, Cabell, Linton, and Ellet) to play golf at East Lake back before World War I.

tem in the lake; I hittem in the woods; I hittem on top; I hittem on the bottom. I hittem everywhere but in the middle. I lose my balls; I lose my money; I lose my temper; I lose my Higher Nature.

I hole out finally at number eighteen, ineffably weary; disappointed, discouraged, disheartened, disgusted, dishonored. I cuss the caddie. I tell him it was all his fault. I dress and go home. I eat my supper. I fuss with the wife and carp at the children. Then I kick the dog and go to bed.

Next morning at the office I tell the boys what a glorious afternoon I had. "You ought to have seen that putt I made on sixteen," I say. Then I turn to my calendar and figure out how many days will elapse before another Wednesday arrives.

Bobby Jones, Golf Master, Dies;
Only Player to Win Grand Slam

ATLANTA. Dec. 18 — Bobby Jones, the master golfer who scored an unparalleled grand slam by winning the United States and British Open and Amateur Tournaments in 1930, died today at his home. His age was 69.

Mr. Jones, a lawyer by profession, who competed only as an amateur, had suffered from a progressive disease of the spinal cord since 1948. By the middle of last December, he was no longer able to go to the offices of his firm, Jones, Bird, & Howell, although he tried to continue working at home. Death came from an aneurysm in his chest. Surviving are his widow, the former Mary Malone; a son, Robert T. 3d of Nashville; two daughters, Mrs. Carl Hood Jr. and Mrs. Clara J. Black; and seven grandchildren.

Bobby Jones in 1930.

Star of a Golden Age
BY FRANK LITSKY

In the decade following World War I, America luxuriated in the Golden Era of Sports and its greatest collection of superathletes: Babe Ruth and Ty Cobb in baseball, Jack Dempsey and Gene Tunney in boxing, Bill Tilden in tennis, Red Grange in football, and Bobby Jones in golf. Many of their records have been broken now, and others are destined to be broken. But one, sports experts agree, may outlast them — Bobby Jones's grand slam of 1930.

Jones, an intense, unspoiled young man, started early on the road to success. At the age of 10, he shot a 90 for 18 holes. At 11 he was down to 80, and at 12 he shot a 70. At 9 he played against men, at 14 he won a major men's tournament, and at 21 he was United States Open champion.

At 28 he achieved the grand slam — victories in one year in the United States Open, British Open, United States Amateur and British Amateur championships. At that point, he retired from tournament golf.

A nation that idolized him for his success grew to respect him even more for his decision to treat golf as a game rather than a way of life. This respect grew with the years.

"First comes my wife and children," he once explained. "Next comes my profession — the law. Finally, and never as a life in itself, comes golf."

His record, aside from the grand slam, was magnificent. He won the United States Open championship four times (1923, 1926, 1929, and 1930), the British Open three times (1926, 1927, and 1930), and the United States Amateur five times (1924, 1925, 1927, 1928, and 1930).

"Jones is as truly the supreme artist as Paderewski is the supreme artist of the piano," George H. Greenfield wrote in *The New York Times* in 1930.

Felt the Tension

Success did not come easily. Though Jones was cool and calculating outwardly, he seethed inside. He could never eat properly during a major tournament. The best his stomach would hold was dry toast and tea.

The pressure of tournament competition manifested itself in other ways, too. Everyone expected Jones to win every time he played, including Atlanta friends who often bet heavily on him. He escaped the unending pressure by retiring from competition.

"Why should I punish myself like this over a golf tournament?" he once asked. "Sometimes I'd pass my mother and dad on the course, look at them and not even see them because I was so concentrated on the game. Afterward, it made a fellow feel a little silly."

The quality of the man projected itself, too. He was worshipped as a national hero in Scotland, the birthplace of golf. Scots would come for miles around to watch him play.

In 1936, on a visit, he made an unannounced trip to the Royal and Ancient Golf Club at St. Andrews for a quiet morning round with friends. There were 5,000 spectators at the first tee and 7,000 at the 18th. Businesses closed as word spread that "Our Bobby is back."

In 1927, when he tapped in his final putt to win the British Open there, an old Scot stood by the green and muttered: "The man canna be human."

Off the course, Jones was convivial in a quiet way. He was a good friend and always the gentleman, though he had full command of strong language when desired. He had a fine sense of humor, and he laughed easily. He smoked cigarettes and drank bourbon.

He was besieged by people who wanted to play a social round of

Jones, at left, with President Eisenhower and Gene Tunney at the White House in 1955.

golf with him. When they talked with him it was always golf. He managed to tolerate their one-sided approach to life. He also learned to put up with the name of Bobby, which he hated (he preferred Bob).

He was not always so serene. As a youngster, he had a reputation for throwing clubs when everything was not going right. When Jim Barnes, the 1921 United States Open champion, watched him let off steam, he said:

"Never mind that club throwing and the beatings he's taking. Defeat will make him great. He's not satisfied now with a pretty good shot. He has to be perfect. That's the

way a good artist must feel."

The defeats Barnes spoke of were frequent in the early years. For young Jones, though he had the game of a man, had the emotions of a growing boy. He never won the big tournaments until he got his temper under control.

At 18, he learned that his greatest opponent was himself. He was playing at Toledo one day with Harry Vardon, the great English professional, and was his usual brash self. They were about even when Jones dribbled a shot into a bunker. Hoping to ease his embarrassment, he turned to Vardon and asked:

"Did you ever see a worse shot?"

"No," replied the crusty Vardon. It was the only word he spoke to Jones all day.

Jones matured, so much so that O.B. Keeler, an Atlanta sports writer and his longtime Boswell, once wrote:

"He has more character than any champion in our history."

He also had the dream of every golfer — a picture swing. No one taught it to him, for he never took a golf lesson in his life. He learned the swing by watching Stewart Maiden, a Scottish professional at the Atlanta Athletic Club course. He would follow Maiden for a few holes, then run home and mimic the swing.

His putting was famous. So was his putter, a rusty, goosenecked club known as Calamity Jane. His strength was driving, putting and an ability to get out of trouble. He was an imaginative player, and he never hesitated to take a chance. In fact, he seldom hesitated on any shot, and he earned an unfair reputation as a mechanical golfer. The game often baffled him. "There are times, " he once said, "when I feel that I know less about what I'm doing on a golf course than anyone else in the world."

When he was an infant, doctors were not sure that he would survive, let alone play golf. He had a serious digestive ailment until he was 5, and he stayed home while other children played. In his later years, he was crippled by syringomyelia, a chronic disease of the spinal cord, and he had circulation and heart trouble.

Robert Tyre Jones, Jr. (named for his grandfather) was born on St. Patrick's Day 1902, in Atlanta. His father was a star outfielder at the University of Georgia, and the youngster's first love was baseball. He also tried tennis. At the age of 9 he settled down to golf.

His parents had taken up the game after moving to a cottage near the East Lake course of the Atlanta Athletic Club. Young Bobby would walk around the course, watch the older folk play, and learn by example. He was only six years old, a scrubby youngster with skinny arms and legs, when he won a six hole tournament. At 9, he was the club's junior champion.

In Philadelphia Tourney

He was 14 when he journeyed to the Merion Cricket Club near Philadelphia for his first United States Amateur championship. He was a chunky lad of 5 feet 4 inches and 165 pounds and somewhat knock-kneed. He was wearing his first pair of long trousers.

After qualifying for match play, he defeated Eben M. Byers, a former champion, in the first round. He beat Frank Dyer, a noted player at the time, in the second round, after losing five of the first six holes. Then he lost to Robert A. Gardner, the defending champion, 5 and 3.

In 1922 he reached the semifinals of the United States Amateur before losing. That ended what he called his seven lean years. Next came what Keeler called "the eight fat years," as Jones finally achieved the heights.

In 1924, Jones decided that he was worrying too much about his opponent in match-play (man against man) competition. He vowed to play for pars and forget about his opponent.

This was a turning point in his career. He started to win match-play competition. That year, at Merion, Pa., he won the United States Amateur for the first time. In the final, he defeated George Von Elm by the overwhelming score of 9 and 8.

Also in 1924, he married Mary Malone, his high school sweetheart.

All this time, golf was a sidelight to education. Jones wanted to be an engineer, and he earned bachelor's and master's degrees in engineering at Georgia Tech. Then he decided to become a lawyer. He went to Harvard and earned another bachelor's degree, then to Emory University in Atlanta for a Bachelor of Laws degree. In 1928, he joined his father's law firm in Atlanta.

In 1929, Jones had a close call in the United States Open at the Winged Foot Golf Club, Mamaroneck, N.Y. He sank a 12-foot sloping, sidehill putt on the last green to tie Al Espinosa. The next day, Jones won their 36-hole title playoff by 23 strokes.

Then came 1930 and the grand slam. Lloyds of London quoted odds of 50 to 1 that Jones wouldn't win the world's four major tournaments that year. He won them.

First came the British Amateur. He started his opening match by shooting 3, 4, 3, and 2. In the final he beat Roger Wethered, 7 and 6. Next was the British Open at Hoylake, England, and his 72-hole score of 291 won that championship.

Back home, Jones got his sternest test of the year in the United States Open at Interlachen near Minneapolis. There were 15,000 spectators in the gallery as he played the par-4 18th hole. He got a birdie 3 by sinking a 40-foot undulating putt, and his 287 won by two strokes.

He had become the first man to win three of the four major titles in one year. The last of the grand slam tournaments, the United States Amateur at Merion, was almost anticlimactic.

No one doubted for the moment that Jones would win. He captured the qualifying medal. He routed Jess Sweetser, 9 and 8, in the semifinal round, and in the final he defeated Gene Homans, 8 and 7. The crowd surged around him so wildly that it took a detachment of United States Marines to get him out safely.

Soon after, he retired from tournament play and made a series of golf motion pictures,the only time he ever made money from the game. Later, he became a vice president of A.G. Spalding & Bros., the sporting goods manufacturer. He became a wealthy lawyer and soft-drink bottler and a business and social leader in Atlanta.

He never played serious tournament golf again. He didn't seem to mind.

"Golf is like eating peanuts," he said. "You can play too much or too little. I've become reconciled to the fact that I'll never play as well as I used to."

A few years later, Jones and the late architect, Alister Mackensie, designed the Augusta National Golf Course in Georgia. In 1934 the Masters tournament was started there and in Jones's lifetime many golf people considered it the most important tournament of all.

Jones played in the first Masters and in

several thereafter, but he was never among the leaders. He always wore his green jacket, signifying club membership, at victory ceremonies, and he served as club president.

He became strong enough to rip a pack of playing cards across the middle, but his health deteriorated. He underwent spinal surgery in 1948 and 1950. He was forced to use one cane, and then two canes, and then a wheelchair, and his weight dropped to less than 100 pounds. He last saw the Masters in 1967.

He was a close friend of Dwight D. Eisenhower, and the President often used his cottage adjacent to the Augusta National course for golfing vacations. During his first term in office, the President painted a 40-by-32 inch oil portrait of Jones at the peak of his game. On the back was printed by hand:

"Bob — from his friend D.D.E., 1953."

In January of 1953, three months after a heart attack, Jones was honored at Golf House, the United States Golf Association headquarters in Manhattan. Augusta National members, including General Eis-

enhower, had donated another oil portrait to be hung at Golf House. A highlight of the ceremony was the reading of a letter from the President.

"Those who have been fortunate enough to know him," the letter said, "realize that his fame as a golfer is transcended by his inestimable qualities as a human being . . . His gift to his friends is the warmth that comes from unselfishness, superb judgement, strength of character, unwavering loyalty to principle."

Bobby Jones listened and cried.

Jones's Route to the Grand Slam

ATLANTA. Dec. 18 (AP) - *Bobby Jones won golf's only grand slam in 1930. Here is how he did it:*

BRITISH AMATEUR
(At St. Andrews, Scotland)

First round: Defeated S.S. Roper, 3 and 2.

Second round: Defeated Cowan Shankland, 5 and 3.

Third round: Defeated G.O. Watt, 7 and 6.

Fourth round: Defeated H.R. Johnston, 1 up.

Fifth round: Defeated Eric Fiddian, 4 and 3.

Semifinals: Defeated George Voigt, 1 up.

Championship, 36 holes: Defeated Roger Wethered, 7 and 6.

BRITISH OPEN
(At Hoylake, England)

Jones won with rounds of 70-72-74-75 — 291, defeating Leo Diegel and Macdonald Smith by two strokes.

U.S. OPEN
(At Interlachen, Minn.)

Jones won with rounds of 71-73-68-75— 287, defeating Macdonald Smith by two strokes.

U.S. AMATEUR
(At Merion, Pa.)

Jones led qualifiers with 69-73 — 142, tying records.

First round: Defeated Ross Somerville, 5 and 4.

Second round: Defeated F.G. Hoblitzel, 5 and 4.

Third round, 36 holes: Defeated Fay Coleman, 6 and 5.

Semifinals, 36 holes: Defeated Jess W. Sweetser, 9 and 8.

Championship: Defeated Gene Homans, 8 and 7.

Returning to Atlanta after taking amateur title in 1924.

Jones is Mourned at Scottish Links
Royal and Ancient Club Flag is Lowered in Memory

ST. ANDREWS, Scotland, Dec. 18 (AP) — The town of St. Andrews and the Royal and Ancient Golf Club, headquarters of the game, mourned the great Bobby Jones today.

Golfers stopped on the Old Course when the news of his death reached them. The flag on the clubhouse was lowered to half staff.

It was on the St. Andrews course that Jones won the British Amateur as part of his grand slam in 1930. Three years earlier he had won the British Open here.

An Honorary Freeman

Later Jones was made an honorary freeman (citizen) of the old town.

The Royal and Ancient Club cabled a message of sympathy to the great golfer's widow.

Keith MacKenzie, secretary of the club, said: "Bobby Jones was an honorary member of this club and his death is a tremendous personal loss to us. We are cabling Mrs. Jones in the name of the captain and members expressing our deepest sorrow."

Mayor Feels His Loss

David Niven, the provost, or mayor, of St. Andrews, said: "What can one say about Bobby Jones? He was a great golfer and the game is poorer for his death. But he was a freeman of St. Andrews, too, and in common with all Scots, we are saddened by the news."

"He was held in great affection by the citizens of St. Andrews."

Arthur Havers, British Open champion in 1923 and an opponent of Jones in many tournaments, said: "He was a wonderful man and all professional golfers held him in esteem. He was always a possible winner in any event he entered. Because of his build he had an unusual style, but it was certainly effective and he was a beautiful putter."

Havers, now 75 years old, once defeated Jones, 2 and 1, in a 36-hole exhibition match.

Jones, with his goose-necked putter, Calamity Jane, after winning the British Open at St. Andrews, Scotland, in 1927.

A LESSON FROM BOBBY JONES

From 1948 until his death in 1971, Bobby Jones experienced progressive weakness of his limbs. It was due to degeneration of the cervical spinal cord (the structure which controls all movement and sensation below the neck).

We know that he suffered through two failed operations on his neck, constant need for help in the simplest motor activities, and had loss of sensation in his arms and legs, which eventually became useless, constantly burning and aching. Cruelest of all, though of enormous inspiration to all who knew him, was the complete sparing of his mind. He taught the world how to win when he was healthy, but his greatest gift to us was his behavior while he was suffering so much.

His life, all of it, is a lesson in behavior. The rest of us will not reach his heights or his fame, but we all will have our little triumphs. Will we be able to shift the spotlight to others by pointing out their achievements? Will we be able to conquer some intrinsic weakness as he controlled his temper? Will we be strong enough to inspire rather than aggravate those who work and live with us and those who must take care of us? Bobby was.

Later in his life Bobby enjoyed fishing, but because of his disease, he had to be helped. Once, at Homosassa in Florida, he was being placed in a boat by a man who worked with him and knew how to handle him. Two old men on the bank watched the awkward process and one turned to the other, thinking they could not be overheard, "I hear he was a great athlete — wonder how he did it, him so crippled an' all." From the boat Bobby cocked his head and smiled at them, "Lots of practice."

His golf was his popular triumph and it reflected his natural talent and determination; but his behavior throughout is the enduring lesson of his life. This is what future generations who study his life will appreciate most. It is his greatest gift to us today.

INDEX

IMPORTANT NAMES, PLACES, AND EVENTS — HOLE BY HOLE

12. A Donald Ross Green — by Rees Jones.
13. Where Jack Nicklaus and Bobby Jones made birdies.
14. Where Miss Joyce Wethered Outdrove Bobby Jones and Charlie Yates in 1935 — She Owned the Swing Bobby Called *"The most perfect in the world."*
15. The Colonel's Most Unusual Tournament.
16. *"A combination of proficiency and profanity."*
17. The End of the Match with Bob Clara in "One Down With One To Play."
18. Bobby's Father, Col. Jones said: *"That drive calls for all there is, in the delicatessen department,"* and Where Twenty-Year-Old Bobby Jones Finished his Course Record Nine Under Par 63, on September 16, 1922.

LIST OF STORIES

THE CONTRIBUTORS
TO THIS BOOK

Tommy Barnes
Dick Boyens
Eugene Branch
Roger Cordes
Richard Courts
Tom Cousins
Mariana Eager
Charlie Elliott
Ed Garner
Jack Glenn, Jr.
Paul Grigsby
Watts Gunn
Scott Hansen
Tom Harding
Charlie Harrison
Harvey Hill
Brem Mayer
Harry McCusker
Charles Steppes, III
Cy Strickler
Edna Wardlaw
Paul Weir
Marion Williams
Ralph Williams
Charlie Yates